Printed in Great Britain
by Amazon.co.uk, Ltd.,
Marston Gate.

NUTRITION GUIDE
FOR CROSSFIT ATHLETES

This book belongs to:

Disclaimer

Before starting any new diet and/or exercise program please check with your doctor and clear any exercise and/or diet changes with them before beginning. I am not a doctor or registered dietitian. I do not provide medical aid or nutrition for the purpose of health or disease and claim to be a doctor or dietitian.

The information in this book is only a summary of the information garnished from the books in the bibliography. I am not liable, either expressly or in an implied manner, nor claim any responsibility for any emotional or physical problems that may occur directly or indirectly from following the recommendations provided in this book.

Again, I am not a nutritionist or dietitian. If you wish to do so please contact a board certified person in your state.

Medical/Health Disclaimer

All information is intended only to help you cooperate with your doctor, in your efforts toward desirable weight levels and health. Only your doctor can determine what is right for you. In addition to regular checkups and medical supervision, from your doctor, before starting any diet or exercise program, you should consult with your personal physician.

All information is generalized, presented for informational purposes only, not medical advice, and presented "as is" without warranty or guarantee of any kind. Readers are cautioned not to rely on this information as medical advice and to consult a qualified medical or dietary professional for their specific needs.

This information is not intended to "diagnose, treat, cure or prevent any disease."

People under treatment for medical conditions or taking medications prescribed by their health care provider should notify their healthcare provider of their planned diet changes because, in some cases, adjustments to medications or modifications to their program may be appropriate.

TABLE OF CONTENTS

How to Use this Book 5

Physical Assessment 6

Overview 7

Food Quality 9

Food Quantity 11

Tips for Preparing Food 17

Nutrition Tracking 18

List of Common Grains to Avoid 195

List of Legumes to Avoid 196

Paleo/Zone Food Blocks 197

Resources 200

"Don't wish it were easier. Wish you were better."

~Jim Rohn

HOW TO USE THIS BOOK

The intention of this book is to provide you with a summary of the nutritional guidelines used by CrossFit trainers and athletes, as well as the tools you need to start and track your progress.

1. Read the book in its entirety.
2. Complete the initial assessment on the next page.
3. Determine your block prescription.
4. Plan your meals.
5. Track your daily progress using the food tracking charts.
6. Update your physical assessment every 30 days and modify your blocks as necessary.

For a video tutorial of the information found in this book, please visit:

http://crossfitlimitless.com/nutrition/

This book is best used in conjunction with our CFL Training Journal:

http://crossfitlimitless.com/training-log/

PHYSICAL ASSESSMENT

	Day 1	Day 30	Day 60	Day 90	Goal
Actual Date:					
Body Weight:					
Body Fat%:					
Measurements					
Neck					
Shoulders					
Chest					
Bicep – R					
Bicep – L					
Waist					
Hips					
Mid-Thigh – R					
Mid-Thigh – L					
Calf – R					
Calf – L					

The CrossFit Method

According to Coach Glassman the hierarchy of concern on which your fitness is built is diet, metabolic conditioning, gymnastics, weightlifting/throwing, and sport, in that order.

Diet lays the molecular foundation of your training. Without proper nutrition you inhibit your body's ability to recover.

What Should I Eat?

Food quality is based on the Paleolithic Diet.

In plain language, eat garden vegetables (especially greens), lean meats, little starch, small amounts of oils, fruits, nuts and seeds. Herbs and natural seasonings are fine for preparing your food.

What Foods Should I Avoid?

Avoid processed foods, foods that contain preservatives, grains, dairy, legumes, and high glycemic carbohydrates.

How Much Should I Eat?

CrossFit follows a Zone Diet, or 30/30/40 ratio, prescription for food quantity.

30% of your caloric intake should come from lean and varied proteins.

30% of your caloric intake should come from monounsaturated fat.

40% of your caloric intake should come from low-glycemic carbohydrates.

You should seek to consume .7 – 1 gram of protein per pound of lean body mass depending on your activity level.

Using Blocks for Portion Control

A block is a unit of measurement for your food portions.

- 1 block of protein = 7 grams of protein
- 1 block of carbohydrates – 9 grams of carbohydrates
- 1 block of fat = 1.5 grams of fat

In order to maintain a 30/30/40 ratio you simply eat an equal number of protein, fat, and carbohydrate blocks at each meal.

A list of Paleo/Zone friendly blocks can be found in the back of this book.

Fluids

Try to consume about 50% of your lean body mass in ounces of water over the course of a day. Limit coffee to 2 cups per day. Avoid sugary drinks like soda and fruit juices.

FOOD QUALITY

Paleo Diet

The Paleo Diet argues that man was designed to be a hunter gatherer. Our bodies were not designed to consume the foods civilized man harvested once we became an agricultural society.

Paleo practitioners point to evidence of diabetes, tooth decay and cancer in Egyptian times. Egyptians were among the first to tame wheat and produce bread. Prior to the Egyptians man died not so much from disease as from exposure, infection, predation or starvation.

Modern science now attributes Western diseases to inflammation. Some foods such as grains, legumes and dairy products can punch through the intestinal tract causing an autoimmune response which results in inflammation. By avoiding these foods we arguably reduce our exposure to inflammation related diseases.

Paleo Foods

Protein sources include lean meats, pork, seafood and eggs.

Carbohydrate sources include vegetables and fruits.

Fats include nuts, oils, animal fat, avocados and olives.

Simple Paleo Prescription

If you're not into weighing and measuring your food, then use the following rule of thumbs to get fast results:

1. Eat 4 meals a day if you're under 180# of lean body mass. Eat 5 meals a day if you're over 185 LBM.
2. Each meal will consist of protein and carbs prepared in a natural oil (olive, avocado, coconut or nut) or animal fat (bacon fat or grass fed lard).
3. The protein size will be about the size of the palm of your hand. The carbs will be 2 large handfuls of vegetables of various

colors. If you don't use oil or fat for cooking, then supplement your diet with some nuts, olives or avocado for fat.

4. Be sure to eat within 30 minutes of working out.
5. Drink half your LBM in water each day.

FOOD QUANTITY

Determining Your Protein Requirement

You only want to eat enough to provide your body with the tools it needs to sustain basic life functions and allow your body to repair itself after intense training sessions. Any excess will be stored for future use as body fat.

1. Determine your lean body mass. Weigh yourself first thing in the morning for best results. Then use either calipers or a bio-electrical impedance device to get your body fat estimate. You can get either for less than $70 on Amazon.com. Subtract your body fat from your total weight to determine your lean body mass (LBM).

2. Multiply your LBM by your activity modifier to determine your daily protein requirement.

Activity Level

Sedentary – no activity	0.5
Light – some walking	0.6
Moderate – exercising at least 3 hours a week	0.7
Active – daily exercise	0.8
Very Active – daily training and heavy weights	0.9
Elite Athlete – daily intense training	1.0

Note: If you CrossFit 4-5 days a week your activity is about a 0.7. If you train 2x daily, then you'd be .8 or .9.

3. Divide your daily protein requirement to determine your block prescription.

Example 1- Male at 200# total weight and 20% body fat who CrossFits 5x weekly.

200 – 20% = 160 LBM

160# LBM x .7 activity modifier = 112 grams of protein daily

112/7 = 16 blocks per day

Example 2- 130# Female at 25% body fat who CrossFits 6 days a week and runs 3-5 miles daily.

130 - 25% = 97.5 LBM

97.5 x .8 activity modifier = 78 gram daily protein requirement

78/7 = 11 blocks per day

Note: The daily block prescription is only a guideline. It serves as a baseline to begin your experimentation. You may need to increase blocks of protein, carbs and/or fat depending on your goals, how you feel and how your body responds.

Planning Your Meals

You'll want to spread your daily block prescription out over the entire day. Some guidelines to follow are:

1. Don't over think this. Most people can spread their blocks out over breakfast, lunch, dinner and a post workout meal.
2. Eat your first meal within 30 minutes of waking, then every 3-4 hours thereafter.
3. Make one of your meals within 30 minutes post workout. This should be your largest meal. Its ok to skip the fat for this meal as fat slows down digestion and you need to start rebuilding while your metabolism is in high gear.
4. If you're hungry you waited too long to eat.
5. If you crave carbs, then you probably ate too many carbs your last meal.
6. Add fat if you feel tired or run down.
7. Add protein if you're not getting stronger week after week.
8. Overeat at least one day a week every two weeks.
9. Choose Paleo friendly foods.

Example 1a - 200# Male with 16 block prescription.

- 7AM Wakeup
- 7:30AM Breakfast – 4 blocks

3 Blocks Protein	3 Blocks Fat	3 Blocks Carbs
3 whole eggs	@ .5 Tbsp. EVOO	1 Banana

- 12PM Lunch – 4 blocks

3 Blocks Protein	3 Blocks Fat	3 Blocks Carbs
3 oz. Grilled Steak	1.5 oz. Avocado	2 cups Roasted Veggies

- 4PM Snack (pre-workout)

2 Blocks Protein	2 Blocks Fat	2 Blocks Carbs
2 oz. Grilled Chicken	6 Almonds	1 Apple

- 6PM Workout
- 7:30PM Post Workout Shake

4 Blocks Protein	0 Blocks Fat	4 Blocks Carbs
1 scoop egg white protein powder.	Skip the fat for this meal.	12 oz. coconut water 1 small banana

- 9:30PM Dinner

4 Blocks Protein	4 Blocks Fat	4 Blocks Carbs
4 oz. Grilled Pork	@ .5 Tbsp. EVOO for salad dressing	1 Sm. Salad 3 oz. Sweet Potato

- 11PM Bed

Example 2a – 130# Female with 11 block prescription.

- 6AM Wake
- 6:30AM Run
- 8AM Post run breakfast – 3 blocks

3 Blocks Protein	3 Blocks Fat	3 Blocks Carbs
3 whole eggs	@ .5 Tbsp. EVOO	1 Banana

- 12PM Lunch – 3 Blocks

3 Blocks Protein	3 Blocks Fat	3 Blocks Carbs
3 oz. Baked Chicken	1.5 oz. Avocado	2 cups Roasted Veggies

- 4PM Pre-Workout Snack – 1 Block

1 Blocks Protein	1 Blocks Fat	1 Blocks Carbs
1 oz. Ham	3 Black Olives	1 Peach

- 6PM Workout
- 7:30PM Post Workout Meal – 3 Blocks

3 Blocks Protein	0 Blocks Fat	3 Blocks Carbs
3 oz. Grilled Steak	Skip the fat for this meal.	3 oz. Sweet Potato

- 8:30PM Snack – 1 Block

1 Blocks Protein	1 Blocks Fat	1 Blocks Carbs
1 oz. Turkey	3 Almonds	1.5 cup Roasted Broccoli

- 11PM Bed

Gaining Weight

If you're looking to gain muscle, then besides increasing your workout volume and poundages, you'll also want to boost your protein and fat intake.

Athletes seem to do well with increasing their activity modifier to 1 – 1.5 grams of LBM while increasing their fat by 3 – 5x.

Losing Weight

To speed the rate at which you lost weight, try increasing your fat by 2 blocks for every 1 block of carbs you remove.

For example, a typical 4 block meal would look like this:

Before:	4B Protein	4B Carbs	4B Fat
After:	4B Protein	2B Carbs	8B Fat

Competition Nutrition

CrossFit competitions are usually comprised of multiple WODs in one day. You need to plan your meals to replenish your body accordingly.

For 3-4 WODs in a day you should use a .8 activity modifier. Stick to carbs like fruits for your carb sources between WODs since their simple sugars are easily accessed.

*"The few who do are the envy of the many
who only watch."*

~ Jim Rohn

1. Prepare a family size pack of pre-measured protein each Sunday and Wednesday. Keep 6 servings worth in the fridge and vacuum seal the rest for storage in your freezer. You'll have a freezer full of ready to eat meat, chicken, fish and pork in no time at all. Then you can stop cooking protein on Wednesdays.

2. Vegetables don't store well, but are easy to prepare, so only make enough for a few days.

3. Buy a scale and vacuum sealer to help prepare your food. Amazon.com or Bed Bath and Beyond carry both.

4. When in doubt, use Calorieking.com to determine the nutrient value of a food.

5. Drink shakes for post workout meals. They're cheap and quick.

6. Most people eat the same 5 or 6 meals. Your goal is to accumulate 5 or 6 "Go-to" meals you can count on day in and day out. Then you can occasionally swap out sides or entrees with new experiments you find on the internet.

7. Use the hand method for measuring portion sizes when eating out (Figure1).

Hand Symbol	Equivalent	Foods	Calories
	Fist 1 cup	Rice, pasta Fruit Veggies	200 75 40
	Palm 3 ounces	Meat Fish Poultry	160 160 160
	Handful 1 ounce	Nuts Raisins	170 85
	2 Handfuls 1 ounce	Chips Popcorn Pretzels	150 120 100
	Thumb 1 ounce	Peanut butter Hard cheese	170 100
	Thumb tip 1 teaspoon	Cooking oil Mayonnaise, butter Sugar	40 35 15

Figure 1

18

Tracking and scoring helps to illustrate your progress and keep you accountable. It also helps you correlate what you are putting in your body and how you feel throughout the day and during workouts. It will help you hone in on the foods your body responds best to. It also allows your coaches to be able to watch your diet and help you fix any initial glitches you might be experiencing with the diet.

You are strongly encouraged to take a "before" photo in your bathing suit to use to compare with your "after" photos to be taken every 30 days. Seeing your transformation will help you stay on track.

Make sure you plan ahead so you aren't stuck in a situation where you are left with no options. A lot of people like to use Sunday to prep for the week. Other people make lunch for the next day at the same time as they are making dinner, so they don't feel like they are spending too much time in the kitchen. Find a system that works and stick to it.

There will be places or situations where you know you have difficulty staying on diet (i.e. at the office working late, where there is an endless supply of bagels, donuts and nothing else) - make sure you have options ready available to you. Talk to your family so they know what you are doing and you don't come home to a meal filled with food you aren't supposed to be eating.

Track your eating on the following is score sheets. From this score sheet you will give yourself a score of 0-10 based on your compliance with the diet. A score of 10 would represent a day of eating like a true hunter gatherer. You score yourself every day.

Not eating your minimum daily protein requirement is an automatic 0 for the day. Results are as follows:

1-6	**Poor**
7-10	Good
11-15	Excellent
16	Elite

Meal/Time	Protein	Carbs	Fat
1.			
2.			
3.			
4.			
5.			

Water: Y/N +1   WOD: Y/N +1   Fish Oil: Y/N +1   Zone: Y/N +3

Penalties: -1 Legumes, -2 Dairy, -3 Grains, -4 Sugary or Fried Food

Deductions:	
Total:	

Start the day with 10 Points: To keep your 10 points you must eat like a true hunter gatherer; nothing but meat, fish, eggs, veggies, fruit, nuts and seeds. Add/subtract bonuses and penalties for total score.

Meal/Time	Protein	Carbs	Fat
1.			
2.			
3.			
4.			
5.			

Water: Y/N +1   WOD: Y/N +1   Fish Oil: Y/N +1   Zone: Y/N +3

Penalties: -1 Legumes, -2 Dairy, -3 Grains, -4 Sugary or Fried Food

Deductions:

Total:

Start the day with 10 Points: To keep your 10 points you must eat like a true hunter gatherer; nothing but meat, fish, eggs, veggies, fruit, nuts and seeds. Add/subtract bonuses and penalties for total score.

Meal/Time	Protein	Carbs	Fat
1.			
2.			
3.			
4.			
5.			

Water: Y/N +1   WOD: Y/N +1   Fish Oil: Y/N +1   Zone: Y/N +3

Penalties: -1 Legumes, -2 Dairy, -3 Grains, -4 Sugary or Fried Food

Deductions:	
Total:	

Start the day with 10 Points: To keep your 10 points you must eat like a true hunter gatherer; nothing but meat, fish, eggs, veggies, fruit, nuts and seeds. Add/subtract bonuses and penalties for total score.

Meal/Time	Protein	Carbs	Fat
1.			
2.			
3.			
4.			
5.			

Water: Y/N +1   WOD: Y/N +1   Fish Oil: Y/N +1   Zone: Y/N +3

Penalties: -1 Legumes, -2 Dairy, -3 Grains, -4 Sugary or Fried Food

Deductions:	
Total:	

Start the day with 10 Points: To keep your 10 points you must eat like a true hunter gatherer; nothing but meat, fish, eggs, veggies, fruit, nuts and seeds. Add/subtract bonuses and penalties for total score.

Meal/Time	Protein	Carbs	Fat
1.			
2.			
3.			
4.			
5.			

Water: Y/N +1   WOD: Y/N +1   Fish Oil: Y/N +1   Zone: Y/N +3

Penalties: -1 Legumes, -2 Dairy, -3 Grains, -4 Sugary or Fried Food

Deductions:	
Total:	

Start the day with 10 Points: To keep your 10 points you must eat like a true hunter gatherer; nothing but meat, fish, eggs, veggies, fruit, nuts and seeds. Add/subtract bonuses and penalties for total score.

Meal/Time	Protein	Carbs	Fat
1.			
2.			
3.			
4.			
5.			

Water: Y/N +1   WOD: Y/N +1   Fish Oil: Y/N +1   Zone: Y/N +3

Penalties: -1 Legumes, -2 Dairy, -3 Grains, -4 Sugary or Fried Food

Deductions:	
Total:	

Start the day with 10 Points: To keep your 10 points you must eat like a true hunter gatherer; nothing but meat, fish, eggs, veggies, fruit, nuts and seeds. Add/subtract bonuses and penalties for total score.

Meal/Time	Protein	Carbs	Fat
1.			
2.			
3.			
4.			
5.			

Water: Y/N +1   WOD: Y/N +1   Fish Oil: Y/N +1   Zone: Y/N +3

Penalties: -1 Legumes, -2 Dairy, -3 Grains, -4 Sugary or Fried Food

Deductions:	
Total:	

Start the day with 10 Points: To keep your 10 points you must eat like a true hunter gatherer; nothing but meat, fish, eggs, veggies, fruit, nuts and seeds. Add/subtract bonuses and penalties for total score.

Meal/Time	Protein	Carbs	Fat
1.			
2.			
3.			
4.			
5.			

Water: Y/N +1   WOD: Y/N +1   Fish Oil: Y/N +1   Zone: Y/N +3

Penalties: -1 Legumes, -2 Dairy, -3 Grains, -4 Sugary or Fried Food

Deductions:	
Total:	

Start the day with 10 Points: To keep your 10 points you must eat like a true hunter gatherer; nothing but meat, fish, eggs, veggies, fruit, nuts and seeds. Add/subtract bonuses and penalties for total score.

Meal/Time	Protein	Carbs	Fat
1.			
2.			
3.			
4.			
5.			

Water: Y/N +1   WOD: Y/N +1   Fish Oil: Y/N +1   Zone: Y/N +3

Penalties: -1 Legumes, -2 Dairy, -3 Grains, -4 Sugary or Fried Food

Deductions:	
Total:	

Start the day with 10 Points: To keep your 10 points you must eat like a true hunter gatherer; nothing but meat, fish, eggs, veggies, fruit, nuts and seeds. Add/subtract bonuses and penalties for total score.

Meal/Time	Protein	Carbs	Fat
1.			
2.			
3.			
4.			
5.			

Water: Y/N +1   WOD: Y/N +1   Fish Oil: Y/N +1   Zone: Y/N +3

Penalties: -1 Legumes, -2 Dairy, -3 Grains, -4 Sugary or Fried Food

Deductions:	
Total:	

Start the day with 10 Points: To keep your 10 points you must eat like a true hunter gatherer; nothing but meat, fish, eggs, veggies, fruit, nuts and seeds. Add/subtract bonuses and penalties for total score.

Meal/Time	Protein	Carbs	Fat
1.			
2.			
3.			
4.			
5.			

Water: Y/N +1   WOD: Y/N +1   Fish Oil: Y/N +1   Zone: Y/N +3

Penalties: -1 Legumes, -2 Dairy, -3 Grains, -4 Sugary or Fried Food

Deductions:	
Total:	

Start the day with 10 Points: To keep your 10 points you must eat like a true hunter gatherer; nothing but meat, fish, eggs, veggies, fruit, nuts and seeds. Add/subtract bonuses and penalties for total score.

Meal/Time	Protein	Carbs	Fat
1.			
2.			
3.			
4.			
5.			

Water: Y/N +1   WOD: Y/N +1   Fish Oil: Y/N +1   Zone: Y/N +3

Penalties: -1 Legumes, -2 Dairy, -3 Grains, -4 Sugary or Fried Food

Deductions:	
Total:	

Start the day with 10 Points: To keep your 10 points you must eat like a true hunter gatherer; nothing but meat, fish, eggs, veggies, fruit, nuts and seeds. Add/subtract bonuses and penalties for total score.

Meal/Time	Protein	Carbs	Fat
1.			
2.			
3.			
4.			
5.			

Water: Y/N +1   WOD: Y/N +1   Fish Oil: Y/N +1   Zone: Y/N +3

Penalties: -1 Legumes, -2 Dairy, -3 Grains, -4 Sugary or Fried Food

Deductions:	
Total:	

Start the day with 10 Points: To keep your 10 points you must eat like a true hunter gatherer; nothing but meat, fish, eggs, veggies, fruit, nuts and seeds. Add/subtract bonuses and penalties for total score.

Meal/Time	Protein	Carbs	Fat
1.			
2.			
3.			
4.			
5.			

Water: Y/N +1   WOD: Y/N +1   Fish Oil: Y/N +1   Zone: Y/N +3

Penalties: -1 Legumes, -2 Dairy, -3 Grains, -4 Sugary or Fried Food

Deductions:	
Total:	

Start the day with 10 Points: To keep your 10 points you must eat like a true hunter gatherer; nothing but meat, fish, eggs, veggies, fruit, nuts and seeds. Add/subtract bonuses and penalties for total score.

Meal/Time	Protein	Carbs	Fat
1.			
2.			
3.			
4.			
5.			

Water: Y/N +1   WOD: Y/N +1   Fish Oil: Y/N +1   Zone: Y/N +3

Penalties: -1 Legumes, -2 Dairy, -3 Grains, -4 Sugary or Fried Food

Deductions:	
Total:	

Start the day with 10 Points: To keep your 10 points you must eat like a true hunter gatherer; nothing but meat, fish, eggs, veggies, fruit, nuts and seeds. Add/subtract bonuses and penalties for total score.

Meal/Time	Protein	Carbs	Fat
1.			
2.			
3.			
4.			
5.			

Water: Y/N +1   WOD: Y/N +1   Fish Oil: Y/N +1   Zone: Y/N +3

Penalties: -1 Legumes, -2 Dairy, -3 Grains, -4 Sugary or Fried Food

Deductions:	
Total:	

Start the day with 10 Points: To keep your 10 points you must eat like a true hunter gatherer; nothing but meat, fish, eggs, veggies, fruit, nuts and seeds. Add/subtract bonuses and penalties for total score.

Meal/Time	Protein	Carbs	Fat
1.			
2.			
3.			
4.			
5.			

Water: Y/N +1   WOD: Y/N +1   Fish Oil: Y/N +1   Zone: Y/N +3

Penalties: -1 Legumes, -2 Dairy, -3 Grains, -4 Sugary or Fried Food

Deductions:	
Total:	

Start the day with 10 Points: To keep your 10 points you must eat like a true hunter gatherer; nothing but meat, fish, eggs, veggies, fruit, nuts and seeds. Add/subtract bonuses and penalties for total score.

Meal/Time	Protein	Carbs	Fat
1.			
2.			
3.			
4.			
5.			

Water: Y/N +1   WOD: Y/N +1   Fish Oil: Y/N +1   Zone: Y/N +3

Penalties: -1 Legumes, -2 Dairy, -3 Grains, -4 Sugary or Fried Food

Deductions:	
Total:	

Start the day with 10 Points: To keep your 10 points you must eat like a true hunter gatherer; nothing but meat, fish, eggs, veggies, fruit, nuts and seeds. Add/subtract bonuses and penalties for total score.

Meal/Time	Protein	Carbs	Fat
1.			
2.			
3.			
4.			
5.			

Water: Y/N +1   WOD: Y/N +1   Fish Oil: Y/N +1   Zone: Y/N +3

Penalties: -1 Legumes, -2 Dairy, -3 Grains, -4 Sugary or Fried Food

Deductions:	
Total:	

Start the day with 10 Points: To keep your 10 points you must eat like a true hunter gatherer; nothing but meat, fish, eggs, veggies, fruit, nuts and seeds. Add/subtract bonuses and penalties for total score.

Meal/Time	Protein	Carbs	Fat
1.			
2.			
3.			
4.			
5.			

Water: Y/N +1   WOD: Y/N +1   Fish Oil: Y/N +1   Zone: Y/N +3

Penalties: -1 Legumes, -2 Dairy, -3 Grains, -4 Sugary or Fried Food

Deductions:	
Total:	

Start the day with 10 Points: To keep your 10 points you must eat like a true hunter gatherer; nothing but meat, fish, eggs, veggies, fruit, nuts and seeds. Add/subtract bonuses and penalties for total score.

Meal/Time	Protein	Carbs	Fat
1.			
2.			
3.			
4.			
5.			

Water: Y/N +1   WOD: Y/N +1   Fish Oil: Y/N +1   Zone: Y/N +3

Penalties: -1 Legumes, -2 Dairy, -3 Grains, -4 Sugary or Fried Food

Deductions:	
Total:	

Start the day with 10 Points: To keep your 10 points you must eat like a true hunter gatherer; nothing but meat, fish, eggs, veggies, fruit, nuts and seeds. Add/subtract bonuses and penalties for total score.

Meal/Time	Protein	Carbs	Fat
1.			
2.			
3.			
4.			
5.			

Water: Y/N +1   WOD: Y/N +1   Fish Oil: Y/N +1   Zone: Y/N +3

Penalties: -1 Legumes, -2 Dairy, -3 Grains, -4 Sugary or Fried Food

Deductions:	
Total:	

Start the day with 10 Points: To keep your 10 points you must eat like a true hunter gatherer; nothing but meat, fish, eggs, veggies, fruit, nuts and seeds. Add/subtract bonuses and penalties for total score.

Meal/Time	Protein	Carbs	Fat
1.			
2.			
3.			
4.			
5.			

Water: Y/N +1   WOD: Y/N +1   Fish Oil: Y/N +1   Zone: Y/N +3

Penalties: -1 Legumes, -2 Dairy, -3 Grains, -4 Sugary or Fried Food

Deductions:	
Total:	

Start the day with 10 Points: To keep your 10 points you must eat like a true hunter gatherer; nothing but meat, fish, eggs, veggies, fruit, nuts and seeds. Add/subtract bonuses and penalties for total score.

Meal/Time	Protein	Carbs	Fat
1.			
2.			
3.			
4.			
5.			

Water: Y/N +1   WOD: Y/N +1   Fish Oil: Y/N +1   Zone: Y/N +3

Penalties: -1 Legumes, -2 Dairy, -3 Grains, -4 Sugary or Fried Food

Deductions:	
Total:	

Start the day with 10 Points: To keep your 10 points you must eat like a true hunter gatherer; nothing but meat, fish, eggs, veggies, fruit, nuts and seeds. Add/subtract bonuses and penalties for total score.

Meal/Time	Protein	Carbs	Fat
1.			
2.			
3.			
4.			
5.			

Water: Y/N +1   WOD: Y/N +1   Fish Oil: Y/N +1   Zone: Y/N +3

Penalties: -1 Legumes, -2 Dairy, -3 Grains, -4 Sugary or Fried Food

Deductions:	
Total:	

Start the day with 10 Points: To keep your 10 points you must eat like a true hunter gatherer; nothing but meat, fish, eggs, veggies, fruit, nuts and seeds. Add/subtract bonuses and penalties for total score.

Meal/Time	Protein	Carbs	Fat
1.			
2.			
3.			
4.			
5.			

Water: Y/N +1   WOD: Y/N +1   Fish Oil: Y/N +1   Zone: Y/N +3

Penalties: -1 Legumes, -2 Dairy, -3 Grains, -4 Sugary or Fried Food

Deductions:	
Total:	

Start the day with 10 Points: To keep your 10 points you must eat like a true hunter gatherer; nothing but meat, fish, eggs, veggies, fruit, nuts and seeds. Add/subtract bonuses and penalties for total score.

Meal/Time	Protein	Carbs	Fat
1.			
2.			
3.			
4.			
5.			

Water: Y/N +1   WOD: Y/N +1   Fish Oil: Y/N +1   Zone: Y/N +3

Penalties: -1 Legumes, -2 Dairy, -3 Grains, -4 Sugary or Fried Food

Deductions:	
Total:	

Start the day with 10 Points: To keep your 10 points you must eat like a true hunter gatherer; nothing but meat, fish, eggs, veggies, fruit, nuts and seeds. Add/subtract bonuses and penalties for total score.

Meal/Time	Protein	Carbs	Fat
1.			
2.			
3.			
4.			
5.			

Water: Y/N +1   WOD: Y/N +1   Fish Oil: Y/N +1   Zone: Y/N +3

Penalties: -1 Legumes, -2 Dairy, -3 Grains, -4 Sugary or Fried Food

Deductions:	
Total:	

Start the day with 10 Points: To keep your 10 points you must eat like a true hunter gatherer; nothing but meat, fish, eggs, veggies, fruit, nuts and seeds. Add/subtract bonuses and penalties for total score.

Meal/Time	Protein	Carbs	Fat
1.			
2.			
3.			
4.			
5.			

Water: Y/N +1   WOD: Y/N +1   Fish Oil: Y/N +1   Zone: Y/N +3

Penalties: -1 Legumes, -2 Dairy, -3 Grains, -4 Sugary or Fried Food

Deductions:	
Total:	

Start the day with 10 Points: To keep your 10 points you must eat like a true hunter gatherer; nothing but meat, fish, eggs, veggies, fruit, nuts and seeds. Add/subtract bonuses and penalties for total score.

Meal/Time	Protein	Carbs	Fat
1.			
2.			
3.			
4.			
5.			

Water: Y/N +1   WOD: Y/N +1   Fish Oil: Y/N +1   Zone: Y/N +3

Penalties: -1 Legumes, -2 Dairy, -3 Grains, -4 Sugary or Fried Food

Deductions:	
Total:	

Start the day with 10 Points: To keep your 10 points you must eat like a true hunter gatherer; nothing but meat, fish, eggs, veggies, fruit, nuts and seeds. Add/subtract bonuses and penalties for total score.

Meal/Time	Protein	Carbs	Fat
1.			
2.			
3.			
4.			
5.			

Water: Y/N +1   WOD: Y/N +1   Fish Oil: Y/N +1   Zone: Y/N +3

Penalties: -1 Legumes, -2 Dairy, -3 Grains, -4 Sugary or Fried Food

Deductions:	
Total:	

Start the day with 10 Points: To keep your 10 points you must eat like a true hunter gatherer; nothing but meat, fish, eggs, veggies, fruit, nuts and seeds. Add/subtract bonuses and penalties for total score.

Meal/Time	Protein	Carbs	Fat
1.			
2.			
3.			
4.			
5.			

Water: Y/N +1   WOD: Y/N +1   Fish Oil: Y/N +1   Zone: Y/N +3

Penalties: -1 Legumes, -2 Dairy, -3 Grains, -4 Sugary or Fried Food

Deductions:	
Total:	

Start the day with 10 Points: To keep your 10 points you must eat like a true hunter gatherer; nothing but meat, fish, eggs, veggies, fruit, nuts and seeds. Add/subtract bonuses and penalties for total score.

Meal/Time	Protein	Carbs	Fat
1.			
2.			
3.			
4.			
5.			

Water: Y/N +1   WOD: Y/N +1   Fish Oil: Y/N +1   Zone: Y/N +3

Penalties: -1 Legumes, -2 Dairy, -3 Grains, -4 Sugary or Fried Food

Deductions:	
Total:	

Start the day with 10 Points: To keep your 10 points you must eat like a true hunter gatherer; nothing but meat, fish, eggs, veggies, fruit, nuts and seeds. Add/subtract bonuses and penalties for total score.

Meal/Time	Protein	Carbs	Fat
1.			
2.			
3.			
4.			
5.			

Water: Y/N +1   WOD: Y/N +1   Fish Oil: Y/N +1   Zone: Y/N +3

Penalties: -1 Legumes, -2 Dairy, -3 Grains, -4 Sugary or Fried Food

Deductions:	
Total:	

Start the day with 10 Points: To keep your 10 points you must eat like a true hunter gatherer; nothing but meat, fish, eggs, veggies, fruit, nuts and seeds. Add/subtract bonuses and penalties for total score.

Meal/Time	Protein	Carbs	Fat
1.			
2.			
3.			
4.			
5.			

Water: Y/N +1   WOD: Y/N +1   Fish Oil: Y/N +1   Zone: Y/N +3

Penalties: -1 Legumes, -2 Dairy, -3 Grains, -4 Sugary or Fried Food

Deductions:	
Total:	

Start the day with 10 Points: To keep your 10 points you must eat like a true hunter gatherer; nothing but meat, fish, eggs, veggies, fruit, nuts and seeds. Add/subtract bonuses and penalties for total score.

Meal/Time	Protein	Carbs	Fat
1.			
2.			
3.			
4.			
5.			

Water: Y/N +1   WOD: Y/N +1   Fish Oil: Y/N +1   Zone: Y/N +3

Penalties: -1 Legumes, -2 Dairy, -3 Grains, -4 Sugary or Fried Food

Deductions:	
Total:	

Start the day with 10 Points: To keep your 10 points you must eat like a true hunter gatherer; nothing but meat, fish, eggs, veggies, fruit, nuts and seeds. Add/subtract bonuses and penalties for total score.

Meal/Time	Protein	Carbs	Fat
1.			
2.			
3.			
4.			
5.			

Water: Y/N +1   WOD: Y/N +1   Fish Oil: Y/N +1   Zone: Y/N +3

Penalties: -1 Legumes, -2 Dairy, -3 Grains, -4 Sugary or Fried Food

Deductions:	
Total:	

Start the day with 10 Points: To keep your 10 points you must eat like a true hunter gatherer; nothing but meat, fish, eggs, veggies, fruit, nuts and seeds. Add/subtract bonuses and penalties for total score.

Meal/Time	Protein	Carbs	Fat
1.			
2.			
3.			
4.			
5.			

Water: Y/N +1   WOD: Y/N +1   Fish Oil: Y/N +1   Zone: Y/N +3

Penalties: -1 Legumes, -2 Dairy, -3 Grains, -4 Sugary or Fried Food

Deductions:	
Total:	

Start the day with 10 Points: To keep your 10 points you must eat like a true hunter gatherer; nothing but meat, fish, eggs, veggies, fruit, nuts and seeds. Add/subtract bonuses and penalties for total score.

Meal/Time	Protein	Carbs	Fat
1.			
2.			
3.			
4.			
5.			

Water: Y/N +1   WOD: Y/N +1   Fish Oil: Y/N +1   Zone: Y/N +3

Penalties: -1 Legumes, -2 Dairy, -3 Grains, -4 Sugary or Fried Food

Deductions:	
Total:	

Start the day with 10 Points: To keep your 10 points you must eat like a true hunter gatherer; nothing but meat, fish, eggs, veggies, fruit, nuts and seeds. Add/subtract bonuses and penalties for total score.

Meal/Time	Protein	Carbs	Fat
1.			
2.			
3.			
4.			
5.			

Water: Y/N +1   WOD: Y/N +1   Fish Oil: Y/N +1   Zone: Y/N +3

Penalties: -1 Legumes, -2 Dairy, -3 Grains, -4 Sugary or Fried Food

Deductions:	
Total:	

Start the day with 10 Points: To keep your 10 points you must eat like a true hunter gatherer; nothing but meat, fish, eggs, veggies, fruit, nuts and seeds. Add/subtract bonuses and penalties for total score.

Meal/Time	Protein	Carbs	Fat
1.			
2.			
3.			
4.			
5.			

Water: Y/N +1   WOD: Y/N +1   Fish Oil: Y/N +1   Zone: Y/N +3

Penalties: -1 Legumes, -2 Dairy, -3 Grains, -4 Sugary or Fried Food

Deductions:

Total:

Start the day with 10 Points: To keep your 10 points you must eat like a true hunter gatherer; nothing but meat, fish, eggs, veggies, fruit, nuts and seeds. Add/subtract bonuses and penalties for total score.

Meal/Time	Protein	Carbs	Fat
1.			
2.			
3.			
4.			
5.			

Water: Y/N +1   WOD: Y/N +1   Fish Oil: Y/N +1   Zone: Y/N +3

Penalties: -1 Legumes, -2 Dairy, -3 Grains, -4 Sugary or Fried Food

Deductions:	
Total:	

Start the day with 10 Points: To keep your 10 points you must eat like a true hunter gatherer; nothing but meat, fish, eggs, veggies, fruit, nuts and seeds. Add/subtract bonuses and penalties for total score.

Meal/Time	Protein	Carbs	Fat
1.			
2.			
3.			
4.			
5.			

Water: Y/N +1   WOD: Y/N +1   Fish Oil: Y/N +1   Zone: Y/N +3

Penalties: -1 Legumes, -2 Dairy, -3 Grains, -4 Sugary or Fried Food

Deductions:	
Total:	

Start the day with 10 Points: To keep your 10 points you must eat like a true hunter gatherer; nothing but meat, fish, eggs, veggies, fruit, nuts and seeds. Add/subtract bonuses and penalties for total score.

Meal/Time	Protein	Carbs	Fat
1.			
2.			
3.			
4.			
5.			

Water: Y/N +1   WOD: Y/N +1   Fish Oil: Y/N +1   Zone: Y/N +3

Penalties: -1 Legumes, -2 Dairy, -3 Grains, -4 Sugary or Fried Food

Deductions:	
Total:	

Start the day with 10 Points: To keep your 10 points you must eat like a true hunter gatherer; nothing but meat, fish, eggs, veggies, fruit, nuts and seeds. Add/subtract bonuses and penalties for total score.

Meal/Time	Protein	Carbs	Fat
1.			
2.			
3.			
4.			
5.			

Water: Y/N +1   WOD: Y/N +1   Fish Oil: Y/N +1   Zone: Y/N +3

Penalties: -1 Legumes, -2 Dairy, -3 Grains, -4 Sugary or Fried Food

Deductions:	
Total:	

Start the day with 10 Points: To keep your 10 points you must eat like a true hunter gatherer; nothing but meat, fish, eggs, veggies, fruit, nuts and seeds. Add/subtract bonuses and penalties for total score.

Meal/Time	Protein	Carbs	Fat
1.			
2.			
3.			
4.			
5.			

Water: Y/N +1   WOD: Y/N +1   Fish Oil: Y/N +1   Zone: Y/N +3

Penalties: -1 Legumes, -2 Dairy, -3 Grains, -4 Sugary or Fried Food

Deductions:	
Total:	

Start the day with 10 Points: To keep your 10 points you must eat like a true hunter gatherer; nothing but meat, fish, eggs, veggies, fruit, nuts and seeds. Add/subtract bonuses and penalties for total score.

Meal/Time	Protein	Carbs	Fat
1.			
2.			
3.			
4.			
5.			

Water: Y/N +1   WOD: Y/N +1   Fish Oil: Y/N +1   Zone: Y/N +3

Penalties: -1 Legumes, -2 Dairy, -3 Grains, -4 Sugary or Fried Food

Deductions:	
Total:	

Start the day with 10 Points: To keep your 10 points you must eat like a true hunter gatherer; nothing but meat, fish, eggs, veggies, fruit, nuts and seeds. Add/subtract bonuses and penalties for total score.

Meal/Time	Protein	Carbs	Fat
1.			
2.			
3.			
4.			
5.			

Water: Y/N +1   WOD: Y/N +1   Fish Oil: Y/N +1   Zone: Y/N +3

Penalties: -1 Legumes, -2 Dairy, -3 Grains, -4 Sugary or Fried Food

Deductions:	
Total:	

Start the day with 10 Points: To keep your 10 points you must eat like a true hunter gatherer; nothing but meat, fish, eggs, veggies, fruit, nuts and seeds. Add/subtract bonuses and penalties for total score.

Meal/Time	Protein	Carbs	Fat
1.			
2.			
3.			
4.			
5.			

Water: Y/N +1   WOD: Y/N +1   Fish Oil: Y/N +1   Zone: Y/N +3

Penalties: -1 Legumes, -2 Dairy, -3 Grains, -4 Sugary or Fried Food

Deductions:	
Total:	

Start the day with 10 Points: To keep your 10 points you must eat like a true hunter gatherer; nothing but meat, fish, eggs, veggies, fruit, nuts and seeds. Add/subtract bonuses and penalties for total score.

Meal/Time	Protein	Carbs	Fat
1.			
2.			
3.			
4.			
5.			

Water: Y/N +1   WOD: Y/N +1   Fish Oil: Y/N +1   Zone: Y/N +3

Penalties: -1 Legumes, -2 Dairy, -3 Grains, -4 Sugary or Fried Food

Deductions:	
Total:	

Start the day with 10 Points: To keep your 10 points you must eat like a true hunter gatherer; nothing but meat, fish, eggs, veggies, fruit, nuts and seeds. Add/subtract bonuses and penalties for total score.

Meal/Time	Protein	Carbs	Fat
1.			
2.			
3.			
4.			
5.			

Water: Y/N +1   WOD: Y/N +1   Fish Oil: Y/N +1   Zone: Y/N +3

Penalties: -1 Legumes, -2 Dairy, -3 Grains, -4 Sugary or Fried Food

Deductions:	
Total:	

Start the day with 10 Points: To keep your 10 points you must eat like a true hunter gatherer; nothing but meat, fish, eggs, veggies, fruit, nuts and seeds. Add/subtract bonuses and penalties for total score.

Meal/Time	Protein	Carbs	Fat
1.			
2.			
3.			
4.			
5.			

Water: Y/N +1   WOD: Y/N +1   Fish Oil: Y/N +1   Zone: Y/N +3

Penalties: -1 Legumes, -2 Dairy, -3 Grains, -4 Sugary or Fried Food

Deductions:	
Total:	

Start the day with 10 Points: To keep your 10 points you must eat like a true hunter gatherer; nothing but meat, fish, eggs, veggies, fruit, nuts and seeds. Add/subtract bonuses and penalties for total score.

Meal/Time	Protein	Carbs	Fat
1.			
2.			
3.			
4.			
5.			

Water: Y/N +1   WOD: Y/N +1   Fish Oil: Y/N +1   Zone: Y/N +3

Penalties: -1 Legumes, -2 Dairy, -3 Grains, -4 Sugary or Fried Food

Deductions:	
Total:	

Start the day with 10 Points: To keep your 10 points you must eat like a true hunter gatherer; nothing but meat, fish, eggs, veggies, fruit, nuts and seeds. Add/subtract bonuses and penalties for total score.

Meal/Time	Protein	Carbs	Fat
1.			
2.			
3.			
4.			
5.			

Water: Y/N +1   WOD: Y/N +1   Fish Oil: Y/N +1   Zone: Y/N +3

Penalties: -1 Legumes, -2 Dairy, -3 Grains, -4 Sugary or Fried Food

Deductions:	
Total:	

Start the day with 10 Points: To keep your 10 points you must eat like a true hunter gatherer; nothing but meat, fish, eggs, veggies, fruit, nuts and seeds. Add/subtract bonuses and penalties for total score.

Meal/Time	Protein	Carbs	Fat
1.			
2.			
3.			
4.			
5.			

Water: Y/N +1   WOD: Y/N +1   Fish Oil: Y/N +1   Zone: Y/N +3

Penalties: -1 Legumes, -2 Dairy, -3 Grains, -4 Sugary or Fried Food

Deductions:	
Total:	

Start the day with 10 Points: To keep your 10 points you must eat like a true hunter gatherer; nothing but meat, fish, eggs, veggies, fruit, nuts and seeds. Add/subtract bonuses and penalties for total score.

Meal/Time	Protein	Carbs	Fat
1.			
2.			
3.			
4.			
5.			

Water: Y/N +1   WOD: Y/N +1   Fish Oil: Y/N +1   Zone: Y/N +3

Penalties: -1 Legumes, -2 Dairy, -3 Grains, -4 Sugary or Fried Food

Deductions:	
Total:	

Start the day with 10 Points: To keep your 10 points you must eat like a true hunter gatherer; nothing but meat, fish, eggs, veggies, fruit, nuts and seeds. Add/subtract bonuses and penalties for total score.

Meal/Time	Protein	Carbs	Fat
1.			
2.			
3.			
4.			
5.			

Water: Y/N +1   WOD: Y/N +1   Fish Oil: Y/N +1   Zone: Y/N +3

Penalties: -1 Legumes, -2 Dairy, -3 Grains, -4 Sugary or Fried Food

Deductions:	
Total:	

Start the day with 10 Points: To keep your 10 points you must eat like a true hunter gatherer; nothing but meat, fish, eggs, veggies, fruit, nuts and seeds. Add/subtract bonuses and penalties for total score.

Meal/Time	Protein	Carbs	Fat
1.			
2.			
3.			
4.			
5.			

Water: Y/N +1   WOD: Y/N +1   Fish Oil: Y/N +1   Zone: Y/N +3

Penalties: -1 Legumes, -2 Dairy, -3 Grains, -4 Sugary or Fried Food

Deductions:	
Total:	

Start the day with 10 Points: To keep your 10 points you must eat like a true hunter gatherer; nothing but meat, fish, eggs, veggies, fruit, nuts and seeds. Add/subtract bonuses and penalties for total score.

Meal/Time	Protein	Carbs	Fat
1.			
2.			
3.			
4.			
5.			

Water: Y/N +1   WOD: Y/N +1   Fish Oil: Y/N +1   Zone: Y/N +3

Penalties: -1 Legumes, -2 Dairy, -3 Grains, -4 Sugary or Fried Food

Deductions:	
Total:	

Start the day with 10 Points: To keep your 10 points you must eat like a true hunter gatherer; nothing but meat, fish, eggs, veggies, fruit, nuts and seeds. Add/subtract bonuses and penalties for total score.

Meal/Time	Protein	Carbs	Fat
1.			
2.			
3.			
4.			
5.			

Water: Y/N +1   WOD: Y/N +1   Fish Oil: Y/N +1   Zone: Y/N +3

Penalties: -1 Legumes, -2 Dairy, -3 Grains, -4 Sugary or Fried Food

Deductions:	
Total:	

Start the day with 10 Points: To keep your 10 points you must eat like a true hunter gatherer; nothing but meat, fish, eggs, veggies, fruit, nuts and seeds. Add/subtract bonuses and penalties for total score.

Meal/Time	Protein	Carbs	Fat
1.			
2.			
3.			
4.			
5.			

Water: Y/N +1   WOD: Y/N +1   Fish Oil: Y/N +1   Zone: Y/N +3

Penalties: -1 Legumes, -2 Dairy, -3 Grains, -4 Sugary or Fried Food

Deductions:	
Total:	

Start the day with 10 Points: To keep your 10 points you must eat like a true hunter gatherer; nothing but meat, fish, eggs, veggies, fruit, nuts and seeds. Add/subtract bonuses and penalties for total score.

Meal/Time	Protein	Carbs	Fat
1.			
2.			
3.			
4.			
5.			

Water: Y/N +1   WOD: Y/N +1   Fish Oil: Y/N +1   Zone: Y/N +3

Penalties: -1 Legumes, -2 Dairy, -3 Grains, -4 Sugary or Fried Food

Deductions:	
Total:	

Start the day with 10 Points: To keep your 10 points you must eat like a true hunter gatherer; nothing but meat, fish, eggs, veggies, fruit, nuts and seeds. Add/subtract bonuses and penalties for total score.

Meal/Time	Protein	Carbs	Fat
1.			
2.			
3.			
4.			
5.			

Water: Y/N +1   WOD: Y/N +1   Fish Oil: Y/N +1   Zone: Y/N +3

Penalties: -1 Legumes, -2 Dairy, -3 Grains, -4 Sugary or Fried Food

Deductions:	
Total:	

Start the day with 10 Points: To keep your 10 points you must eat like a true hunter gatherer; nothing but meat, fish, eggs, veggies, fruit, nuts and seeds. Add/subtract bonuses and penalties for total score.

Meal/Time	Protein	Carbs	Fat
1.			
2.			
3.			
4.			
5.			

Water: Y/N +1   WOD: Y/N +1   Fish Oil: Y/N +1   Zone: Y/N +3

Penalties: -1 Legumes, -2 Dairy, -3 Grains, -4 Sugary or Fried Food

Deductions:	
Total:	

Start the day with 10 Points: To keep your 10 points you must eat like a true hunter gatherer; nothing but meat, fish, eggs, veggies, fruit, nuts and seeds. Add/subtract bonuses and penalties for total score.

Meal/Time	Protein	Carbs	Fat
1.			
2.			
3.			
4.			
5.			

Water: Y/N +1   WOD: Y/N +1   Fish Oil: Y/N +1   Zone: Y/N +3

Penalties: -1 Legumes, -2 Dairy, -3 Grains, -4 Sugary or Fried Food

Deductions:	
Total:	

Start the day with 10 Points: To keep your 10 points you must eat like a true hunter gatherer; nothing but meat, fish, eggs, veggies, fruit, nuts and seeds. Add/subtract bonuses and penalties for total score.

Meal/Time	Protein	Carbs	Fat
1.			
2.			
3.			
4.			
5.			

Water: Y/N +1   WOD: Y/N +1   Fish Oil: Y/N +1   Zone: Y/N +3

Penalties: -1 Legumes, -2 Dairy, -3 Grains, -4 Sugary or Fried Food

Deductions:	
Total:	

Start the day with 10 Points: To keep your 10 points you must eat like a true hunter gatherer; nothing but meat, fish, eggs, veggies, fruit, nuts and seeds. Add/subtract bonuses and penalties for total score.

Meal/Time	Protein	Carbs	Fat
1.			
2.			
3.			
4.			
5.			

Water: Y/N +1   WOD: Y/N +1   Fish Oil: Y/N +1   Zone: Y/N +3

Penalties: -1 Legumes, -2 Dairy, -3 Grains, -4 Sugary or Fried Food

Deductions:	
Total:	

Start the day with 10 Points: To keep your 10 points you must eat like a true hunter gatherer; nothing but meat, fish, eggs, veggies, fruit, nuts and seeds. Add/subtract bonuses and penalties for total score.

Meal/Time	Protein	Carbs	Fat
1.			
2.			
3.			
4.			
5.			

Water: Y/N +1   WOD: Y/N +1   Fish Oil: Y/N +1   Zone: Y/N +3

Penalties: -1 Legumes, -2 Dairy, -3 Grains, -4 Sugary or Fried Food

Deductions:	
Total:	

Start the day with 10 Points: To keep your 10 points you must eat like a true hunter gatherer; nothing but meat, fish, eggs, veggies, fruit, nuts and seeds. Add/subtract bonuses and penalties for total score.

Meal/Time	Protein	Carbs	Fat
1.			
2.			
3.			
4.			
5.			

Water: Y/N +1   WOD: Y/N +1   Fish Oil: Y/N +1   Zone: Y/N +3

Penalties: -1 Legumes, -2 Dairy, -3 Grains, -4 Sugary or Fried Food

Deductions:	
Total:	

Start the day with 10 Points: To keep your 10 points you must eat like a true hunter gatherer; nothing but meat, fish, eggs, veggies, fruit, nuts and seeds. Add/subtract bonuses and penalties for total score.

Meal/Time	Protein	Carbs	Fat
1.			
2.			
3.			
4.			
5.			

Water: Y/N +1   WOD: Y/N +1   Fish Oil: Y/N +1   Zone: Y/N +3

Penalties: -1 Legumes, -2 Dairy, -3 Grains, -4 Sugary or Fried Food

Deductions:	
Total:	

Start the day with 10 Points: To keep your 10 points you must eat like a true hunter gatherer; nothing but meat, fish, eggs, veggies, fruit, nuts and seeds. Add/subtract bonuses and penalties for total score.

Meal/Time	Protein	Carbs	Fat
1.			
2.			
3.			
4.			
5.			

Water: Y/N +1   WOD: Y/N +1   Fish Oil: Y/N +1   Zone: Y/N +3

Penalties: -1 Legumes, -2 Dairy, -3 Grains, -4 Sugary or Fried Food

Deductions:	
Total:	

Start the day with 10 Points: To keep your 10 points you must eat like a true hunter gatherer; nothing but meat, fish, eggs, veggies, fruit, nuts and seeds. Add/subtract bonuses and penalties for total score.

Meal/Time	Protein	Carbs	Fat
1.			
2.			
3.			
4.			
5.			

Water: Y/N +1   WOD: Y/N +1   Fish Oil: Y/N +1   Zone: Y/N +3

Penalties: -1 Legumes, -2 Dairy, -3 Grains, -4 Sugary or Fried Food

Deductions:	
Total:	

Start the day with 10 Points: To keep your 10 points you must eat like a true hunter gatherer; nothing but meat, fish, eggs, veggies, fruit, nuts and seeds. Add/subtract bonuses and penalties for total score.

Meal/Time	Protein	Carbs	Fat
1.			
2.			
3.			
4.			
5.			

Water: Y/N +1   WOD: Y/N +1   Fish Oil: Y/N +1   Zone: Y/N +3

Penalties: -1 Legumes, -2 Dairy, -3 Grains, -4 Sugary or Fried Food

Deductions:	
Total:	

Start the day with 10 Points: To keep your 10 points you must eat like a true hunter gatherer; nothing but meat, fish, eggs, veggies, fruit, nuts and seeds. Add/subtract bonuses and penalties for total score.

Meal/Time	Protein	Carbs	Fat
1.			
2.			
3.			
4.			
5.			

Water: Y/N +1   WOD: Y/N +1   Fish Oil: Y/N +1   Zone: Y/N +3

Penalties: -1 Legumes, -2 Dairy, -3 Grains, -4 Sugary or Fried Food

Deductions:	
Total:	

Start the day with 10 Points: To keep your 10 points you must eat like a true hunter gatherer; nothing but meat, fish, eggs, veggies, fruit, nuts and seeds. Add/subtract bonuses and penalties for total score.

Meal/Time	Protein	Carbs	Fat
1.			
2.			
3.			
4.			
5.			

Water: Y/N +1   WOD: Y/N +1   Fish Oil: Y/N +1   Zone: Y/N +3

Penalties: -1 Legumes, -2 Dairy, -3 Grains, -4 Sugary or Fried Food

Deductions:	
Total:	

Start the day with 10 Points: To keep your 10 points you must eat like a true hunter gatherer; nothing but meat, fish, eggs, veggies, fruit, nuts and seeds. Add/subtract bonuses and penalties for total score.

Meal/Time	Protein	Carbs	Fat
1.			
2.			
3.			
4.			
5.			

Water: Y/N +1   WOD: Y/N +1   Fish Oil: Y/N +1   Zone: Y/N +3

Penalties: -1 Legumes, -2 Dairy, -3 Grains, -4 Sugary or Fried Food

Deductions:	
Total:	

Start the day with 10 Points: To keep your 10 points you must eat like a true hunter gatherer; nothing but meat, fish, eggs, veggies, fruit, nuts and seeds. Add/subtract bonuses and penalties for total score.

Meal/Time	Protein	Carbs	Fat
1.			
2.			
3.			
4.			
5.			

Water: Y/N +1   WOD: Y/N +1   Fish Oil: Y/N +1   Zone: Y/N +3

Penalties: -1 Legumes, -2 Dairy, -3 Grains, -4 Sugary or Fried Food

Deductions:	
Total:	

Start the day with 10 Points: To keep your 10 points you must eat like a true hunter gatherer; nothing but meat, fish, eggs, veggies, fruit, nuts and seeds. Add/subtract bonuses and penalties for total score.

Meal/Time	Protein	Carbs	Fat
1.			
2.			
3.			
4.			
5.			

Water: Y/N +1   WOD: Y/N +1   Fish Oil: Y/N +1   Zone: Y/N +3

Penalties: -1 Legumes, -2 Dairy, -3 Grains, -4 Sugary or Fried Food

Deductions:	
Total:	

Start the day with 10 Points: To keep your 10 points you must eat like a true hunter gatherer; nothing but meat, fish, eggs, veggies, fruit, nuts and seeds. Add/subtract bonuses and penalties for total score.

Meal/Time	Protein	Carbs	Fat
1.			
2.			
3.			
4.			
5.			

Water: Y/N +1   WOD: Y/N +1   Fish Oil: Y/N +1   Zone: Y/N +3

Penalties: -1 Legumes, -2 Dairy, -3 Grains, -4 Sugary or Fried Food

Deductions:

Total:

Start the day with 10 Points: To keep your 10 points you must eat like a true hunter gatherer; nothing but meat, fish, eggs, veggies, fruit, nuts and seeds. Add/subtract bonuses and penalties for total score.

Meal/Time	Protein	Carbs	Fat
1.			
2.			
3.			
4.			
5.			

Water: Y/N +1   WOD: Y/N +1   Fish Oil: Y/N +1   Zone: Y/N +3

Penalties: -1 Legumes, -2 Dairy, -3 Grains, -4 Sugary or Fried Food

Deductions:	
Total:	

Start the day with 10 Points: To keep your 10 points you must eat like a true hunter gatherer; nothing but meat, fish, eggs, veggies, fruit, nuts and seeds. Add/subtract bonuses and penalties for total score.

Meal/Time	Protein	Carbs	Fat
1.			
2.			
3.			
4.			
5.			

Water: Y/N +1   WOD: Y/N +1   Fish Oil: Y/N +1   Zone: Y/N +3

Penalties: -1 Legumes, -2 Dairy, -3 Grains, -4 Sugary or Fried Food

Deductions:	
Total:	

Start the day with 10 Points: To keep your 10 points you must eat like a true hunter gatherer; nothing but meat, fish, eggs, veggies, fruit, nuts and seeds. Add/subtract bonuses and penalties for total score.

Meal/Time	Protein	Carbs	Fat
1.			
2.			
3.			
4.			
5.			

Water: Y/N +1   WOD: Y/N +1   Fish Oil: Y/N +1   Zone: Y/N +3

Penalties: -1 Legumes, -2 Dairy, -3 Grains, -4 Sugary or Fried Food

Deductions:	
Total:	

Start the day with 10 Points: To keep your 10 points you must eat like a true hunter gatherer; nothing but meat, fish, eggs, veggies, fruit, nuts and seeds. Add/subtract bonuses and penalties for total score.

Meal/Time	Protein	Carbs	Fat
1.			
2.			
3.			
4.			
5.			

Water: Y/N +1   WOD: Y/N +1   Fish Oil: Y/N +1   Zone: Y/N +3

Penalties: -1 Legumes, -2 Dairy, -3 Grains, -4 Sugary or Fried Food

Deductions:	
Total:	

Start the day with 10 Points: To keep your 10 points you must eat like a true hunter gatherer; nothing but meat, fish, eggs, veggies, fruit, nuts and seeds. Add/subtract bonuses and penalties for total score.

Meal/Time	Protein	Carbs	Fat
1.			
2.			
3.			
4.			
5.			

Water: Y/N +1   WOD: Y/N +1   Fish Oil: Y/N +1   Zone: Y/N +3

Penalties: -1 Legumes, -2 Dairy, -3 Grains, -4 Sugary or Fried Food

Deductions:	
Total:	

Start the day with 10 Points: To keep your 10 points you must eat like a true hunter gatherer; nothing but meat, fish, eggs, veggies, fruit, nuts and seeds. Add/subtract bonuses and penalties for total score.

Meal/Time	Protein	Carbs	Fat
1.			
2.			
3.			
4.			
5.			

Water: Y/N +1   WOD: Y/N +1   Fish Oil: Y/N +1   Zone: Y/N +3

Penalties: -1 Legumes, -2 Dairy, -3 Grains, -4 Sugary or Fried Food

Deductions:	
Total:	

Start the day with 10 Points: To keep your 10 points you must eat like a true hunter gatherer; nothing but meat, fish, eggs, veggies, fruit, nuts and seeds. Add/subtract bonuses and penalties for total score.

Meal/Time	Protein	Carbs	Fat
1.			
2.			
3.			
4.			
5.			

Water: Y/N +1   WOD: Y/N +1   Fish Oil: Y/N +1   Zone: Y/N +3

Penalties: -1 Legumes, -2 Dairy, -3 Grains, -4 Sugary or Fried Food

Deductions:	
Total:	

Start the day with 10 Points: To keep your 10 points you must eat like a true hunter gatherer; nothing but meat, fish, eggs, veggies, fruit, nuts and seeds. Add/subtract bonuses and penalties for total score.

Meal/Time	Protein	Carbs	Fat
1.			
2.			
3.			
4.			
5.			

Water: Y/N +1   WOD: Y/N +1   Fish Oil: Y/N +1   Zone: Y/N +3

Penalties: -1 Legumes, -2 Dairy, -3 Grains, -4 Sugary or Fried Food

Deductions:	
Total:	

Start the day with 10 Points: To keep your 10 points you must eat like a true hunter gatherer; nothing but meat, fish, eggs, veggies, fruit, nuts and seeds. Add/subtract bonuses and penalties for total score.

Meal/Time	Protein	Carbs	Fat
1.			
2.			
3.			
4.			
5.			

Water: Y/N +1   WOD: Y/N +1   Fish Oil: Y/N +1   Zone: Y/N +3

Penalties: -1 Legumes, -2 Dairy, -3 Grains, -4 Sugary or Fried Food

Deductions:	
Total:	

Start the day with 10 Points: To keep your 10 points you must eat like a true hunter gatherer; nothing but meat, fish, eggs, veggies, fruit, nuts and seeds. Add/subtract bonuses and penalties for total score.

Meal/Time	Protein	Carbs	Fat
1.			
2.			
3.			
4.			
5.			

Water: Y/N +1   WOD: Y/N +1   Fish Oil: Y/N +1   Zone: Y/N +3

Penalties: -1 Legumes, -2 Dairy, -3 Grains, -4 Sugary or Fried Food

Deductions:	
Total:	

Start the day with 10 Points: To keep your 10 points you must eat like a true hunter gatherer; nothing but meat, fish, eggs, veggies, fruit, nuts and seeds. Add/subtract bonuses and penalties for total score.

Meal/Time	Protein	Carbs	Fat
1.			
2.			
3.			
4.			
5.			

Water: Y/N +1   WOD: Y/N +1   Fish Oil: Y/N +1   Zone: Y/N +3

Penalties: -1 Legumes, -2 Dairy, -3 Grains, -4 Sugary or Fried Food

Deductions:	
Total:	

Start the day with 10 Points: To keep your 10 points you must eat like a true hunter gatherer; nothing but meat, fish, eggs, veggies, fruit, nuts and seeds. Add/subtract bonuses and penalties for total score.

Meal/Time	Protein	Carbs	Fat
1.			
2.			
3.			
4.			
5.			

Water: Y/N +1   WOD: Y/N +1   Fish Oil: Y/N +1   Zone: Y/N +3

Penalties: -1 Legumes, -2 Dairy, -3 Grains, -4 Sugary or Fried Food

Deductions:	
Total:	

Start the day with 10 Points: To keep your 10 points you must eat like a true hunter gatherer; nothing but meat, fish, eggs, veggies, fruit, nuts and seeds. Add/subtract bonuses and penalties for total score.

Meal/Time	Protein	Carbs	Fat
1.			
2.			
3.			
4.			
5.			

Water: Y/N +1   WOD: Y/N +1   Fish Oil: Y/N +1   Zone: Y/N +3

Penalties: -1 Legumes, -2 Dairy, -3 Grains, -4 Sugary or Fried Food

Deductions:	
Total:	

Start the day with 10 Points: To keep your 10 points you must eat like a true hunter gatherer; nothing but meat, fish, eggs, veggies, fruit, nuts and seeds. Add/subtract bonuses and penalties for total score.

Meal/Time	Protein	Carbs	Fat
1.			
2.			
3.			
4.			
5.			

Water: Y/N +1   WOD: Y/N +1   Fish Oil: Y/N +1   Zone: Y/N +3

Penalties: -1 Legumes, -2 Dairy, -3 Grains, -4 Sugary or Fried Food

Deductions:	
Total:	

Start the day with 10 Points: To keep your 10 points you must eat like a true hunter gatherer; nothing but meat, fish, eggs, veggies, fruit, nuts and seeds. Add/subtract bonuses and penalties for total score.

Meal/Time	Protein	Carbs	Fat
1.			
2.			
3.			
4.			
5.			

Water: Y/N +1   WOD: Y/N +1   Fish Oil: Y/N +1   Zone: Y/N +3

Penalties: -1 Legumes, -2 Dairy, -3 Grains, -4 Sugary or Fried Food

Deductions:	
Total:	

Start the day with 10 Points: To keep your 10 points you must eat like a true hunter gatherer; nothing but meat, fish, eggs, veggies, fruit, nuts and seeds. Add/subtract bonuses and penalties for total score.

Meal/Time	Protein	Carbs	Fat
1.			
2.			
3.			
4.			
5.			

Water: Y/N +1   WOD: Y/N +1   Fish Oil: Y/N +1   Zone: Y/N +3

Penalties: -1 Legumes, -2 Dairy, -3 Grains, -4 Sugary or Fried Food

Deductions:	
Total:	

Start the day with 10 Points: To keep your 10 points you must eat like a true hunter gatherer; nothing but meat, fish, eggs, veggies, fruit, nuts and seeds. Add/subtract bonuses and penalties for total score.

Meal/Time	Protein	Carbs	Fat
1.			
2.			
3.			
4.			
5.			

Water: Y/N +1   WOD: Y/N +1   Fish Oil: Y/N +1   Zone: Y/N +3

Penalties: -1 Legumes, -2 Dairy, -3 Grains, -4 Sugary or Fried Food

Deductions:	
Total:	

Start the day with 10 Points: To keep your 10 points you must eat like a true hunter gatherer; nothing but meat, fish, eggs, veggies, fruit, nuts and seeds. Add/subtract bonuses and penalties for total score.

Meal/Time	Protein	Carbs	Fat
1.			
2.			
3.			
4.			
5.			

Water: Y/N +1   WOD: Y/N +1   Fish Oil: Y/N +1   Zone: Y/N +3

Penalties: -1 Legumes, -2 Dairy, -3 Grains, -4 Sugary or Fried Food

Deductions:	
Total:	

Start the day with 10 Points: To keep your 10 points you must eat like a true hunter gatherer; nothing but meat, fish, eggs, veggies, fruit, nuts and seeds. Add/subtract bonuses and penalties for total score.

Meal/Time	Protein	Carbs	Fat
1.			
2.			
3.			
4.			
5.			

Water: Y/N +1   WOD: Y/N +1   Fish Oil: Y/N +1   Zone: Y/N +3

Penalties: -1 Legumes, -2 Dairy, -3 Grains, -4 Sugary or Fried Food

Deductions:	
Total:	

Start the day with 10 Points: To keep your 10 points you must eat like a true hunter gatherer; nothing but meat, fish, eggs, veggies, fruit, nuts and seeds. Add/subtract bonuses and penalties for total score.

Meal/Time	Protein	Carbs	Fat
1.			
2.			
3.			
4.			
5.			

Water: Y/N +1   WOD: Y/N +1   Fish Oil: Y/N +1   Zone: Y/N +3

Penalties: -1 Legumes, -2 Dairy, -3 Grains, -4 Sugary or Fried Food

Deductions:	
Total:	

Start the day with 10 Points: To keep your 10 points you must eat like a true hunter gatherer; nothing but meat, fish, eggs, veggies, fruit, nuts and seeds. Add/subtract bonuses and penalties for total score.

Meal/Time	Protein	Carbs	Fat
1.			
2.			
3.			
4.			
5.			

Water: Y/N +1   WOD: Y/N +1   Fish Oil: Y/N +1   Zone: Y/N +3

Penalties: -1 Legumes, -2 Dairy, -3 Grains, -4 Sugary or Fried Food

Deductions:	
Total:	

Start the day with 10 Points: To keep your 10 points you must eat like a true hunter gatherer; nothing but meat, fish, eggs, veggies, fruit, nuts and seeds. Add/subtract bonuses and penalties for total score.

Meal/Time	Protein	Carbs	Fat
1.			
2.			
3.			
4.			
5.			

Water: Y/N +1   WOD: Y/N +1   Fish Oil: Y/N +1   Zone: Y/N +3

Penalties: -1 Legumes, -2 Dairy, -3 Grains, -4 Sugary or Fried Food

Deductions:	
Total:	

Start the day with 10 Points: To keep your 10 points you must eat like a true hunter gatherer; nothing but meat, fish, eggs, veggies, fruit, nuts and seeds. Add/subtract bonuses and penalties for total score.

Meal/Time	Protein	Carbs	Fat
1.			
2.			
3.			
4.			
5.			

Water: Y/N +1   WOD: Y/N +1   Fish Oil: Y/N +1   Zone: Y/N +3

Penalties: -1 Legumes, -2 Dairy, -3 Grains, -4 Sugary or Fried Food

Deductions:	
Total:	

Start the day with 10 Points: To keep your 10 points you must eat like a true hunter gatherer; nothing but meat, fish, eggs, veggies, fruit, nuts and seeds. Add/subtract bonuses and penalties for total score.

Meal/Time	Protein	Carbs	Fat
1.			
2.			
3.			
4.			
5.			

Water: Y/N +1   WOD: Y/N +1   Fish Oil: Y/N +1   Zone: Y/N +3

Penalties: -1 Legumes, -2 Dairy, -3 Grains, -4 Sugary or Fried Food

Deductions:	
Total:	

Start the day with 10 Points: To keep your 10 points you must eat like a true hunter gatherer; nothing but meat, fish, eggs, veggies, fruit, nuts and seeds. Add/subtract bonuses and penalties for total score.

Meal/Time	Protein	Carbs	Fat
1.			
2.			
3.			
4.			
5.			

Water: Y/N +1   WOD: Y/N +1   Fish Oil: Y/N +1   Zone: Y/N +3

Penalties: -1 Legumes, -2 Dairy, -3 Grains, -4 Sugary or Fried Food

Deductions:	
Total:	

Start the day with 10 Points: To keep your 10 points you must eat like a true hunter gatherer; nothing but meat, fish, eggs, veggies, fruit, nuts and seeds. Add/subtract bonuses and penalties for total score.

Meal/Time	Protein	Carbs	Fat
1.			
2.			
3.			
4.			
5.			

Water: Y/N +1   WOD: Y/N +1   Fish Oil: Y/N +1   Zone: Y/N +3

Penalties: -1 Legumes, -2 Dairy, -3 Grains, -4 Sugary or Fried Food

Deductions:	
Total:	

Start the day with 10 Points: To keep your 10 points you must eat like a true hunter gatherer; nothing but meat, fish, eggs, veggies, fruit, nuts and seeds. Add/subtract bonuses and penalties for total score.

Meal/Time	Protein	Carbs	Fat
1.			
2.			
3.			
4.			
5.			

Water: Y/N +1   WOD: Y/N +1   Fish Oil: Y/N +1   Zone: Y/N +3

Penalties: -1 Legumes, -2 Dairy, -3 Grains, -4 Sugary or Fried Food

Deductions:	
Total:	

Start the day with 10 Points: To keep your 10 points you must eat like a true hunter gatherer; nothing but meat, fish, eggs, veggies, fruit, nuts and seeds. Add/subtract bonuses and penalties for total score.

Meal/Time	Protein	Carbs	Fat
1.			
2.			
3.			
4.			
5.			

Water: Y/N +1   WOD: Y/N +1   Fish Oil: Y/N +1   Zone: Y/N +3

Penalties: -1 Legumes, -2 Dairy, -3 Grains, -4 Sugary or Fried Food

Deductions:	
Total:	

Start the day with 10 Points: To keep your 10 points you must eat like a true hunter gatherer; nothing but meat, fish, eggs, veggies, fruit, nuts and seeds. Add/subtract bonuses and penalties for total score.

Meal/Time	Protein	Carbs	Fat
1.			
2.			
3.			
4.			
5.			

Water: Y/N +1   WOD: Y/N +1   Fish Oil: Y/N +1   Zone: Y/N +3

Penalties: -1 Legumes, -2 Dairy, -3 Grains, -4 Sugary or Fried Food

Deductions:	
Total:	

Start the day with 10 Points: To keep your 10 points you must eat like a true hunter gatherer; nothing but meat, fish, eggs, veggies, fruit, nuts and seeds. Add/subtract bonuses and penalties for total score.

Meal/Time	Protein	Carbs	Fat
1.			
2.			
3.			
4.			
5.			

Water: Y/N +1   WOD: Y/N +1   Fish Oil: Y/N +1   Zone: Y/N +3

Penalties: -1 Legumes, -2 Dairy, -3 Grains, -4 Sugary or Fried Food

Deductions:	
Total:	

Start the day with 10 Points: To keep your 10 points you must eat like a true hunter gatherer; nothing but meat, fish, eggs, veggies, fruit, nuts and seeds. Add/subtract bonuses and penalties for total score.

Meal/Time	Protein	Carbs	Fat
1.			
2.			
3.			
4.			
5.			

Water: Y/N +1   WOD: Y/N +1   Fish Oil: Y/N +1   Zone: Y/N +3

Penalties: -1 Legumes, -2 Dairy, -3 Grains, -4 Sugary or Fried Food

Deductions:	
Total:	

Start the day with 10 Points: To keep your 10 points you must eat like a true hunter gatherer; nothing but meat, fish, eggs, veggies, fruit, nuts and seeds. Add/subtract bonuses and penalties for total score.

Meal/Time	Protein	Carbs	Fat
1.			
2.			
3.			
4.			
5.			

Water: Y/N +1   WOD: Y/N +1   Fish Oil: Y/N +1   Zone: Y/N +3

Penalties: -1 Legumes, -2 Dairy, -3 Grains, -4 Sugary or Fried Food

Deductions:	
Total:	

Start the day with 10 Points: To keep your 10 points you must eat like a true hunter gatherer; nothing but meat, fish, eggs, veggies, fruit, nuts and seeds. Add/subtract bonuses and penalties for total score.

Meal/Time	Protein	Carbs	Fat
1.			
2.			
3.			
4.			
5.			

Water: Y/N +1   WOD: Y/N +1   Fish Oil: Y/N +1   Zone: Y/N +3

Penalties: -1 Legumes, -2 Dairy, -3 Grains, -4 Sugary or Fried Food

Deductions:	
Total:	

Start the day with 10 Points: To keep your 10 points you must eat like a true hunter gatherer; nothing but meat, fish, eggs, veggies, fruit, nuts and seeds. Add/subtract bonuses and penalties for total score.

Meal/Time	Protein	Carbs	Fat
1.			
2.			
3.			
4.			
5.			

Water: Y/N +1   WOD: Y/N +1   Fish Oil: Y/N +1   Zone: Y/N +3

Penalties: -1 Legumes, -2 Dairy, -3 Grains, -4 Sugary or Fried Food

Deductions:	
Total:	

Start the day with 10 Points: To keep your 10 points you must eat like a true hunter gatherer; nothing but meat, fish, eggs, veggies, fruit, nuts and seeds. Add/subtract bonuses and penalties for total score.

Meal/Time	Protein	Carbs	Fat
1.			
2.			
3.			
4.			
5.			

Water: Y/N +1   WOD: Y/N +1   Fish Oil: Y/N +1   Zone: Y/N +3

Penalties: -1 Legumes, -2 Dairy, -3 Grains, -4 Sugary or Fried Food

Deductions:	
Total:	

Start the day with 10 Points: To keep your 10 points you must eat like a true hunter gatherer; nothing but meat, fish, eggs, veggies, fruit, nuts and seeds. Add/subtract bonuses and penalties for total score.

Meal/Time	Protein	Carbs	Fat
1.			
2.			
3.			
4.			
5.			

Water: Y/N +1   WOD: Y/N +1   Fish Oil: Y/N +1   Zone: Y/N +3

Penalties: -1 Legumes, -2 Dairy, -3 Grains, -4 Sugary or Fried Food

Deductions:	
Total:	

Start the day with 10 Points: To keep your 10 points you must eat like a true hunter gatherer; nothing but meat, fish, eggs, veggies, fruit, nuts and seeds. Add/subtract bonuses and penalties for total score.

Meal/Time	Protein	Carbs	Fat
1.			
2.			
3.			
4.			
5.			

Water: Y/N +1   WOD: Y/N +1   Fish Oil: Y/N +1   Zone: Y/N +3

Penalties: -1 Legumes, -2 Dairy, -3 Grains, -4 Sugary or Fried Food

Deductions:	
Total:	

Start the day with 10 Points: To keep your 10 points you must eat like a true hunter gatherer; nothing but meat, fish, eggs, veggies, fruit, nuts and seeds. Add/subtract bonuses and penalties for total score.

Meal/Time	Protein	Carbs	Fat
1.			
2.			
3.			
4.			
5.			

Water: Y/N +1   WOD: Y/N +1   Fish Oil: Y/N +1   Zone: Y/N +3

Penalties: -1 Legumes, -2 Dairy, -3 Grains, -4 Sugary or Fried Food

Deductions:	
Total:	

Start the day with 10 Points: To keep your 10 points you must eat like a true hunter gatherer; nothing but meat, fish, eggs, veggies, fruit, nuts and seeds. Add/subtract bonuses and penalties for total score.

Meal/Time	Protein	Carbs	Fat
1.			
2.			
3.			
4.			
5.			

Water: Y/N +1   WOD: Y/N +1   Fish Oil: Y/N +1   Zone: Y/N +3

Penalties: -1 Legumes, -2 Dairy, -3 Grains, -4 Sugary or Fried Food

Deductions:	
Total:	

Start the day with 10 Points: To keep your 10 points you must eat like a true hunter gatherer; nothing but meat, fish, eggs, veggies, fruit, nuts and seeds. Add/subtract bonuses and penalties for total score.

Meal/Time	Protein	Carbs	Fat
1.			
2.			
3.			
4.			
5.			

Water: Y/N +1   WOD: Y/N +1   Fish Oil: Y/N +1   Zone: Y/N +3

Penalties: -1 Legumes, -2 Dairy, -3 Grains, -4 Sugary or Fried Food

Deductions:	
Total:	

Start the day with 10 Points: To keep your 10 points you must eat like a true hunter gatherer; nothing but meat, fish, eggs, veggies, fruit, nuts and seeds. Add/subtract bonuses and penalties for total score.

Meal/Time	Protein	Carbs	Fat
1.			
2.			
3.			
4.			
5.			

Water: Y/N +1   WOD: Y/N +1   Fish Oil: Y/N +1   Zone: Y/N +3

Penalties: -1 Legumes, -2 Dairy, -3 Grains, -4 Sugary or Fried Food

Deductions:	
Total:	

Start the day with 10 Points: To keep your 10 points you must eat like a true hunter gatherer; nothing but meat, fish, eggs, veggies, fruit, nuts and seeds. Add/subtract bonuses and penalties for total score.

Meal/Time	Protein	Carbs	Fat
1.			
2.			
3.			
4.			
5.			

Water: Y/N +1   WOD: Y/N +1   Fish Oil: Y/N +1   Zone: Y/N +3

Penalties: -1 Legumes, -2 Dairy, -3 Grains, -4 Sugary or Fried Food

Deductions:	
Total:	

Start the day with 10 Points: To keep your 10 points you must eat like a true hunter gatherer; nothing but meat, fish, eggs, veggies, fruit, nuts and seeds. Add/subtract bonuses and penalties for total score.

Meal/Time	Protein	Carbs	Fat
1.			
2.			
3.			
4.			
5.			

Water: Y/N +1   WOD: Y/N +1   Fish Oil: Y/N +1   Zone: Y/N +3

Penalties: -1 Legumes, -2 Dairy, -3 Grains, -4 Sugary or Fried Food

Deductions:	
Total:	

Start the day with 10 Points: To keep your 10 points you must eat like a true hunter gatherer; nothing but meat, fish, eggs, veggies, fruit, nuts and seeds. Add/subtract bonuses and penalties for total score.

Meal/Time	Protein	Carbs	Fat
1.			
2.			
3.			
4.			
5.			

Water: Y/N +1   WOD: Y/N +1   Fish Oil: Y/N +1   Zone: Y/N +3

Penalties: -1 Legumes, -2 Dairy, -3 Grains, -4 Sugary or Fried Food

Deductions:	
Total:	

Start the day with 10 Points: To keep your 10 points you must eat like a true hunter gatherer; nothing but meat, fish, eggs, veggies, fruit, nuts and seeds. Add/subtract bonuses and penalties for total score.

Meal/Time	Protein	Carbs	Fat
1.			
2.			
3.			
4.			
5.			

Water: Y/N +1   WOD: Y/N +1   Fish Oil: Y/N +1   Zone: Y/N +3

Penalties: -1 Legumes, -2 Dairy, -3 Grains, -4 Sugary or Fried Food

Deductions:	
Total:	

Start the day with 10 Points: To keep your 10 points you must eat like a true hunter gatherer; nothing but meat, fish, eggs, veggies, fruit, nuts and seeds. Add/subtract bonuses and penalties for total score.

Meal/Time	Protein	Carbs	Fat
1.			
2.			
3.			
4.			
5.			

Water: Y/N +1   WOD: Y/N +1   Fish Oil: Y/N +1   Zone: Y/N +3

Penalties: -1 Legumes, -2 Dairy, -3 Grains, -4 Sugary or Fried Food

Deductions:	
Total:	

Start the day with 10 Points: To keep your 10 points you must eat like a true hunter gatherer; nothing but meat, fish, eggs, veggies, fruit, nuts and seeds. Add/subtract bonuses and penalties for total score.

Meal/Time	Protein	Carbs	Fat
1.			
2.			
3.			
4.			
5.			

Water: Y/N +1   WOD: Y/N +1   Fish Oil: Y/N +1   Zone: Y/N +3

Penalties: -1 Legumes, -2 Dairy, -3 Grains, -4 Sugary or Fried Food

Deductions:	
Total:	

Start the day with 10 Points: To keep your 10 points you must eat like a true hunter gatherer; nothing but meat, fish, eggs, veggies, fruit, nuts and seeds. Add/subtract bonuses and penalties for total score.

Meal/Time	Protein	Carbs	Fat
1.			
2.			
3.			
4.			
5.			

Water: Y/N +1   WOD: Y/N +1   Fish Oil: Y/N +1   Zone: Y/N +3

Penalties: -1 Legumes, -2 Dairy, -3 Grains, -4 Sugary or Fried Food

Deductions:	
Total:	

Start the day with 10 Points: To keep your 10 points you must eat like a true hunter gatherer; nothing but meat, fish, eggs, veggies, fruit, nuts and seeds. Add/subtract bonuses and penalties for total score.

Meal/Time	Protein	Carbs	Fat
1.			
2.			
3.			
4.			
5.			

Water: Y/N +1   WOD: Y/N +1   Fish Oil: Y/N +1   Zone: Y/N +3

Penalties: -1 Legumes, -2 Dairy, -3 Grains, -4 Sugary or Fried Food

Deductions:	
Total:	

Start the day with 10 Points: To keep your 10 points you must eat like a true hunter gatherer; nothing but meat, fish, eggs, veggies, fruit, nuts and seeds. Add/subtract bonuses and penalties for total score.

Meal/Time	Protein	Carbs	Fat
1.			
2.			
3.			
4.			
5.			

Water: Y/N +1   WOD: Y/N +1   Fish Oil: Y/N +1   Zone: Y/N +3

Penalties: -1 Legumes, -2 Dairy, -3 Grains, -4 Sugary or Fried Food

Deductions:	
Total:	

Start the day with 10 Points: To keep your 10 points you must eat like a true hunter gatherer; nothing but meat, fish, eggs, veggies, fruit, nuts and seeds. Add/subtract bonuses and penalties for total score.

Meal/Time	Protein	Carbs	Fat
1.			
2.			
3.			
4.			
5.			

Water: Y/N +1   WOD: Y/N +1   Fish Oil: Y/N +1   Zone: Y/N +3

Penalties: -1 Legumes, -2 Dairy, -3 Grains, -4 Sugary or Fried Food

Deductions:	
Total:	

Start the day with 10 Points: To keep your 10 points you must eat like a true hunter gatherer; nothing but meat, fish, eggs, veggies, fruit, nuts and seeds. Add/subtract bonuses and penalties for total score.

Meal/Time	Protein	Carbs	Fat
1.			
2.			
3.			
4.			
5.			

Water: Y/N +1   WOD: Y/N +1   Fish Oil: Y/N +1   Zone: Y/N +3

Penalties: -1 Legumes, -2 Dairy, -3 Grains, -4 Sugary or Fried Food

Deductions:	
Total:	

Start the day with 10 Points: To keep your 10 points you must eat like a true hunter gatherer; nothing but meat, fish, eggs, veggies, fruit, nuts and seeds. Add/subtract bonuses and penalties for total score.

Meal/Time	Protein	Carbs	Fat
1.			
2.			
3.			
4.			
5.			

Water: Y/N +1   WOD: Y/N +1   Fish Oil: Y/N +1   Zone: Y/N +3

Penalties: -1 Legumes, -2 Dairy, -3 Grains, -4 Sugary or Fried Food

Deductions:	
Total:	

Start the day with 10 Points: To keep your 10 points you must eat like a true hunter gatherer; nothing but meat, fish, eggs, veggies, fruit, nuts and seeds. Add/subtract bonuses and penalties for total score.

Meal/Time	Protein	Carbs	Fat
1.			
2.			
3.			
4.			
5.			

Water: Y/N +1   WOD: Y/N +1   Fish Oil: Y/N +1   Zone: Y/N +3

Penalties: -1 Legumes, -2 Dairy, -3 Grains, -4 Sugary or Fried Food

Deductions:	
Total:	

Start the day with 10 Points: To keep your 10 points you must eat like a true hunter gatherer; nothing but meat, fish, eggs, veggies, fruit, nuts and seeds. Add/subtract bonuses and penalties for total score.

Meal/Time	Protein	Carbs	Fat
1.			
2.			
3.			
4.			
5.			

Water: Y/N +1   WOD: Y/N +1   Fish Oil: Y/N +1   Zone: Y/N +3

Penalties: -1 Legumes, -2 Dairy, -3 Grains, -4 Sugary or Fried Food

Deductions:	
Total:	

Start the day with 10 Points: To keep your 10 points you must eat like a true hunter gatherer; nothing but meat, fish, eggs, veggies, fruit, nuts and seeds. Add/subtract bonuses and penalties for total score.

Meal/Time	Protein	Carbs	Fat
1.			
2.			
3.			
4.			
5.			

Water: Y/N +1   WOD: Y/N +1   Fish Oil: Y/N +1   Zone: Y/N +3

Penalties: -1 Legumes, -2 Dairy, -3 Grains, -4 Sugary or Fried Food

Deductions:	
Total:	

Start the day with 10 Points: To keep your 10 points you must eat like a true hunter gatherer; nothing but meat, fish, eggs, veggies, fruit, nuts and seeds. Add/subtract bonuses and penalties for total score.

Meal/Time	Protein	Carbs	Fat
1.			
2.			
3.			
4.			
5.			

Water: Y/N +1   WOD: Y/N +1   Fish Oil: Y/N +1   Zone: Y/N +3

Penalties: -1 Legumes, -2 Dairy, -3 Grains, -4 Sugary or Fried Food

Deductions:	
Total:	

Start the day with 10 Points: To keep your 10 points you must eat like a true hunter gatherer; nothing but meat, fish, eggs, veggies, fruit, nuts and seeds. Add/subtract bonuses and penalties for total score.

Meal/Time	Protein	Carbs	Fat
1.			
2.			
3.			
4.			
5.			

Water: Y/N +1   WOD: Y/N +1   Fish Oil: Y/N +1   Zone: Y/N +3

Penalties: -1 Legumes, -2 Dairy, -3 Grains, -4 Sugary or Fried Food

Deductions:	
Total:	

Start the day with 10 Points: To keep your 10 points you must eat like a true hunter gatherer; nothing but meat, fish, eggs, veggies, fruit, nuts and seeds. Add/subtract bonuses and penalties for total score.

Meal/Time	Protein	Carbs	Fat
1.			
2.			
3.			
4.			
5.			

Water: Y/N +1   WOD: Y/N +1   Fish Oil: Y/N +1   Zone: Y/N +3

Penalties: -1 Legumes, -2 Dairy, -3 Grains, -4 Sugary or Fried Food

Deductions:	
Total:	

Start the day with 10 Points: To keep your 10 points you must eat like a true hunter gatherer; nothing but meat, fish, eggs, veggies, fruit, nuts and seeds. Add/subtract bonuses and penalties for total score.

Meal/Time	Protein	Carbs	Fat
1.			
2.			
3.			
4.			
5.			

Water: Y/N +1   WOD: Y/N +1   Fish Oil: Y/N +1   Zone: Y/N +3

Penalties: -1 Legumes, -2 Dairy, -3 Grains, -4 Sugary or Fried Food

Deductions:	
Total:	

Start the day with 10 Points: To keep your 10 points you must eat like a true hunter gatherer; nothing but meat, fish, eggs, veggies, fruit, nuts and seeds. Add/subtract bonuses and penalties for total score.

Meal/Time	Protein	Carbs	Fat
1.			
2.			
3.			
4.			
5.			

Water: Y/N +1   WOD: Y/N +1   Fish Oil: Y/N +1   Zone: Y/N +3

Penalties: -1 Legumes, -2 Dairy, -3 Grains, -4 Sugary or Fried Food

Deductions:	
Total:	

Start the day with 10 Points: To keep your 10 points you must eat like a true hunter gatherer; nothing but meat, fish, eggs, veggies, fruit, nuts and seeds. Add/subtract bonuses and penalties for total score.

Meal/Time	Protein	Carbs	Fat
1.			
2.			
3.			
4.			
5.			

Water: Y/N +1   WOD: Y/N +1   Fish Oil: Y/N +1   Zone: Y/N +3

Penalties: -1 Legumes, -2 Dairy, -3 Grains, -4 Sugary or Fried Food

Deductions:	
Total:	

Start the day with 10 Points: To keep your 10 points you must eat like a true hunter gatherer; nothing but meat, fish, eggs, veggies, fruit, nuts and seeds. Add/subtract bonuses and penalties for total score.

Meal/Time	Protein	Carbs	Fat
1.			
2.			
3.			
4.			
5.			

Water: Y/N +1   WOD: Y/N +1   Fish Oil: Y/N +1   Zone: Y/N +3

Penalties: -1 Legumes, -2 Dairy, -3 Grains, -4 Sugary or Fried Food

Deductions:	
Total:	

Start the day with 10 Points: To keep your 10 points you must eat like a true hunter gatherer; nothing but meat, fish, eggs, veggies, fruit, nuts and seeds. Add/subtract bonuses and penalties for total score.

Meal/Time	Protein	Carbs	Fat
1.			
2.			
3.			
4.			
5.			

Water: Y/N +1   WOD: Y/N +1   Fish Oil: Y/N +1   Zone: Y/N +3

Penalties: -1 Legumes, -2 Dairy, -3 Grains, -4 Sugary or Fried Food

Deductions:	
Total:	

Start the day with 10 Points: To keep your 10 points you must eat like a true hunter gatherer; nothing but meat, fish, eggs, veggies, fruit, nuts and seeds. Add/subtract bonuses and penalties for total score.

Meal/Time	Protein	Carbs	Fat
1.			
2.			
3.			
4.			
5.			

Water: Y/N +1   WOD: Y/N +1   Fish Oil: Y/N +1   Zone: Y/N +3

Penalties: -1 Legumes, -2 Dairy, -3 Grains, -4 Sugary or Fried Food

Deductions:	
Total:	

Start the day with 10 Points: To keep your 10 points you must eat like a true hunter gatherer; nothing but meat, fish, eggs, veggies, fruit, nuts and seeds. Add/subtract bonuses and penalties for total score.

Meal/Time	Protein	Carbs	Fat
1.			
2.			
3.			
4.			
5.			

Water: Y/N +1   WOD: Y/N +1   Fish Oil: Y/N +1   Zone: Y/N +3

Penalties: -1 Legumes, -2 Dairy, -3 Grains, -4 Sugary or Fried Food

Deductions:	
Total:	

Start the day with 10 Points: To keep your 10 points you must eat like a true hunter gatherer; nothing but meat, fish, eggs, veggies, fruit, nuts and seeds. Add/subtract bonuses and penalties for total score.

Meal/Time	Protein	Carbs	Fat
1.			
2.			
3.			
4.			
5.			

Water: Y/N +1   WOD: Y/N +1   Fish Oil: Y/N +1   Zone: Y/N +3

Penalties: -1 Legumes, -2 Dairy, -3 Grains, -4 Sugary or Fried Food

Deductions:	
Total:	

Start the day with 10 Points: To keep your 10 points you must eat like a true hunter gatherer; nothing but meat, fish, eggs, veggies, fruit, nuts and seeds. Add/subtract bonuses and penalties for total score.

Meal/Time	Protein	Carbs	Fat
1.			
2.			
3.			
4.			
5.			

Water: Y/N +1   WOD: Y/N +1   Fish Oil: Y/N +1   Zone: Y/N +3

Penalties: -1 Legumes, -2 Dairy, -3 Grains, -4 Sugary or Fried Food

Deductions:	
Total:	

Start the day with 10 Points: To keep your 10 points you must eat like a true hunter gatherer; nothing but meat, fish, eggs, veggies, fruit, nuts and seeds. Add/subtract bonuses and penalties for total score.

Meal/Time	Protein	Carbs	Fat
1.			
2.			
3.			
4.			
5.			

Water: Y/N +1   WOD: Y/N +1   Fish Oil: Y/N +1   Zone: Y/N +3

Penalties: -1 Legumes, -2 Dairy, -3 Grains, -4 Sugary or Fried Food

Deductions:	
Total:	

Start the day with 10 Points: To keep your 10 points you must eat like a true hunter gatherer; nothing but meat, fish, eggs, veggies, fruit, nuts and seeds. Add/subtract bonuses and penalties for total score.

Meal/Time	Protein	Carbs	Fat
1.			
2.			
3.			
4.			
5.			

Water: Y/N +1   WOD: Y/N +1   Fish Oil: Y/N +1   Zone: Y/N +3

Penalties: -1 Legumes, -2 Dairy, -3 Grains, -4 Sugary or Fried Food

Deductions:	
Total:	

Start the day with 10 Points: To keep your 10 points you must eat like a true hunter gatherer; nothing but meat, fish, eggs, veggies, fruit, nuts and seeds. Add/subtract bonuses and penalties for total score.

Meal/Time	Protein	Carbs	Fat
1.			
2.			
3.			
4.			
5.			

Water: Y/N +1   WOD: Y/N +1   Fish Oil: Y/N +1   Zone: Y/N +3

Penalties: -1 Legumes, -2 Dairy, -3 Grains, -4 Sugary or Fried Food

Deductions:	
Total:	

Start the day with 10 Points: To keep your 10 points you must eat like a true hunter gatherer; nothing but meat, fish, eggs, veggies, fruit, nuts and seeds. Add/subtract bonuses and penalties for total score.

Meal/Time	Protein	Carbs	Fat
1.			
2.			
3.			
4.			
5.			

Water: Y/N +1   WOD: Y/N +1   Fish Oil: Y/N +1   Zone: Y/N +3

Penalties: -1 Legumes, -2 Dairy, -3 Grains, -4 Sugary or Fried Food

Deductions:	
Total:	

Start the day with 10 Points: To keep your 10 points you must eat like a true hunter gatherer; nothing but meat, fish, eggs, veggies, fruit, nuts and seeds. Add/subtract bonuses and penalties for total score.

Meal/Time	Protein	Carbs	Fat
1.			
2.			
3.			
4.			
5.			

Water: Y/N +1   WOD: Y/N +1   Fish Oil: Y/N +1   Zone: Y/N +3

Penalties: -1 Legumes, -2 Dairy, -3 Grains, -4 Sugary or Fried Food

Deductions:	
Total:	

Start the day with 10 Points: To keep your 10 points you must eat like a true hunter gatherer; nothing but meat, fish, eggs, veggies, fruit, nuts and seeds. Add/subtract bonuses and penalties for total score.

Meal/Time	Protein	Carbs	Fat
1.			
2.			
3.			
4.			
5.			

Water: Y/N +1   WOD: Y/N +1   Fish Oil: Y/N +1   Zone: Y/N +3

Penalties: -1 Legumes, -2 Dairy, -3 Grains, -4 Sugary or Fried Food

Deductions:	
Total:	

Start the day with 10 Points: To keep your 10 points you must eat like a true hunter gatherer; nothing but meat, fish, eggs, veggies, fruit, nuts and seeds. Add/subtract bonuses and penalties for total score.

Meal/Time	Protein	Carbs	Fat
1.			
2.			
3.			
4.			
5.			

Water: Y/N +1   WOD: Y/N +1   Fish Oil: Y/N +1   Zone: Y/N +3

Penalties: -1 Legumes, -2 Dairy, -3 Grains, -4 Sugary or Fried Food

Deductions:	
Total:	

Start the day with 10 Points: To keep your 10 points you must eat like a true hunter gatherer; nothing but meat, fish, eggs, veggies, fruit, nuts and seeds. Add/subtract bonuses and penalties for total score.

Meal/Time	Protein	Carbs	Fat
1.			
2.			
3.			
4.			
5.			

Water: Y/N +1   WOD: Y/N +1   Fish Oil: Y/N +1   Zone: Y/N +3

Penalties: -1 Legumes, -2 Dairy, -3 Grains, -4 Sugary or Fried Food

Deductions:	
Total:	

Start the day with 10 Points: To keep your 10 points you must eat like a true hunter gatherer; nothing but meat, fish, eggs, veggies, fruit, nuts and seeds. Add/subtract bonuses and penalties for total score.

Meal/Time	Protein	Carbs	Fat
1.			
2.			
3.			
4.			
5.			

Water: Y/N +1   WOD: Y/N +1   Fish Oil: Y/N +1   Zone: Y/N +3

Penalties: -1 Legumes, -2 Dairy, -3 Grains, -4 Sugary or Fried Food

Deductions:	
Total:	

Start the day with 10 Points: To keep your 10 points you must eat like a true hunter gatherer; nothing but meat, fish, eggs, veggies, fruit, nuts and seeds. Add/subtract bonuses and penalties for total score.

Meal/Time	Protein	Carbs	Fat
1.			
2.			
3.			
4.			
5.			

Water: Y/N +1   WOD: Y/N +1   Fish Oil: Y/N +1   Zone: Y/N +3

Penalties: -1 Legumes, -2 Dairy, -3 Grains, -4 Sugary or Fried Food

Deductions:	
Total:	

Start the day with 10 Points: To keep your 10 points you must eat like a true hunter gatherer; nothing but meat, fish, eggs, veggies, fruit, nuts and seeds. Add/subtract bonuses and penalties for total score.

Meal/Time	Protein	Carbs	Fat
1.			
2.			
3.			
4.			
5.			

Water: Y/N +1   WOD: Y/N +1   Fish Oil: Y/N +1   Zone: Y/N +3

Penalties: -1 Legumes, -2 Dairy, -3 Grains, -4 Sugary or Fried Food

Deductions:	
Total:	

Start the day with 10 Points: To keep your 10 points you must eat like a true hunter gatherer; nothing but meat, fish, eggs, veggies, fruit, nuts and seeds. Add/subtract bonuses and penalties for total score.

Meal/Time	Protein	Carbs	Fat
1.			
2.			
3.			
4.			
5.			

Water: Y/N +1   WOD: Y/N +1   Fish Oil: Y/N +1   Zone: Y/N +3

Penalties: -1 Legumes, -2 Dairy, -3 Grains, -4 Sugary or Fried Food

Deductions:	
Total:	

Start the day with 10 Points: To keep your 10 points you must eat like a true hunter gatherer; nothing but meat, fish, eggs, veggies, fruit, nuts and seeds. Add/subtract bonuses and penalties for total score.

Meal/Time	Protein	Carbs	Fat
1.			
2.			
3.			
4.			
5.			

Water: Y/N +1   WOD: Y/N +1   Fish Oil: Y/N +1   Zone: Y/N +3

Penalties: -1 Legumes, -2 Dairy, -3 Grains, -4 Sugary or Fried Food

Deductions:	
Total:	

Start the day with 10 Points: To keep your 10 points you must eat like a true hunter gatherer; nothing but meat, fish, eggs, veggies, fruit, nuts and seeds. Add/subtract bonuses and penalties for total score.

Meal/Time	Protein	Carbs	Fat
1.			
2.			
3.			
4.			
5.			

Water: Y/N +1   WOD: Y/N +1   Fish Oil: Y/N +1   Zone: Y/N +3

Penalties: -1 Legumes, -2 Dairy, -3 Grains, -4 Sugary or Fried Food

Deductions:	
Total:	

Start the day with 10 Points: To keep your 10 points you must eat like a true hunter gatherer; nothing but meat, fish, eggs, veggies, fruit, nuts and seeds. Add/subtract bonuses and penalties for total score.

Meal/Time	Protein	Carbs	Fat
1.			
2.			
3.			
4.			
5.			

Water: Y/N +1   WOD: Y/N +1   Fish Oil: Y/N +1   Zone: Y/N +3

Penalties: -1 Legumes, -2 Dairy, -3 Grains, -4 Sugary or Fried Food

Deductions:	
Total:	

Start the day with 10 Points: To keep your 10 points you must eat like a true hunter gatherer; nothing but meat, fish, eggs, veggies, fruit, nuts and seeds. Add/subtract bonuses and penalties for total score.

Meal/Time	Protein	Carbs	Fat
1.			
2.			
3.			
4.			
5.			

Water: Y/N +1   WOD: Y/N +1   Fish Oil: Y/N +1   Zone: Y/N +3

Penalties: -1 Legumes, -2 Dairy, -3 Grains, -4 Sugary or Fried Food

Deductions:	
Total:	

Start the day with 10 Points: To keep your 10 points you must eat like a true hunter gatherer; nothing but meat, fish, eggs, veggies, fruit, nuts and seeds. Add/subtract bonuses and penalties for total score.

Meal/Time	Protein	Carbs	Fat
1.			
2.			
3.			
4.			
5.			

Water: Y/N +1   WOD: Y/N +1   Fish Oil: Y/N +1   Zone: Y/N +3

Penalties: -1 Legumes, -2 Dairy, -3 Grains, -4 Sugary or Fried Food

Deductions:	
Total:	

Start the day with 10 Points: To keep your 10 points you must eat like a true hunter gatherer; nothing but meat, fish, eggs, veggies, fruit, nuts and seeds. Add/subtract bonuses and penalties for total score.

Meal/Time	Protein	Carbs	Fat
1.			
2.			
3.			
4.			
5.			

Water: Y/N +1   WOD: Y/N +1   Fish Oil: Y/N +1   Zone: Y/N +3

Penalties: -1 Legumes, -2 Dairy, -3 Grains, -4 Sugary or Fried Food

Deductions:	
Total:	

Start the day with 10 Points: To keep your 10 points you must eat like a true hunter gatherer; nothing but meat, fish, eggs, veggies, fruit, nuts and seeds. Add/subtract bonuses and penalties for total score.

Meal/Time	Protein	Carbs	Fat
1.			
2.			
3.			
4.			
5.			

Water: Y/N +1   WOD: Y/N +1   Fish Oil: Y/N +1   Zone: Y/N +3

Penalties: -1 Legumes, -2 Dairy, -3 Grains, -4 Sugary or Fried Food

Deductions:	
Total:	

Start the day with 10 Points: To keep your 10 points you must eat like a true hunter gatherer; nothing but meat, fish, eggs, veggies, fruit, nuts and seeds. Add/subtract bonuses and penalties for total score.

Meal/Time	Protein	Carbs	Fat
1.			
2.			
3.			
4.			
5.			

Water: Y/N +1   WOD: Y/N +1   Fish Oil: Y/N +1   Zone: Y/N +3

Penalties: -1 Legumes, -2 Dairy, -3 Grains, -4 Sugary or Fried Food

Deductions:	
Total:	

Start the day with 10 Points: To keep your 10 points you must eat like a true hunter gatherer; nothing but meat, fish, eggs, veggies, fruit, nuts and seeds. Add/subtract bonuses and penalties for total score.

Meal/Time	Protein	Carbs	Fat
1.			
2.			
3.			
4.			
5.			

Water: Y/N +1   WOD: Y/N +1   Fish Oil: Y/N +1   Zone: Y/N +3

Penalties: -1 Legumes, -2 Dairy, -3 Grains, -4 Sugary or Fried Food

Deductions:	
Total:	

Start the day with 10 Points: To keep your 10 points you must eat like a true hunter gatherer; nothing but meat, fish, eggs, veggies, fruit, nuts and seeds. Add/subtract bonuses and penalties for total score.

Meal/Time	Protein	Carbs	Fat
1.			
2.			
3.			
4.			
5.			

Water: Y/N +1   WOD: Y/N +1   Fish Oil: Y/N +1   Zone: Y/N +3

Penalties: -1 Legumes, -2 Dairy, -3 Grains, -4 Sugary or Fried Food

Deductions:	
Total:	

Start the day with 10 Points: To keep your 10 points you must eat like a true hunter gatherer; nothing but meat, fish, eggs, veggies, fruit, nuts and seeds. Add/subtract bonuses and penalties for total score.

Meal/Time	Protein	Carbs	Fat
1.			
2.			
3.			
4.			
5.			

Water: Y/N +1   WOD: Y/N +1   Fish Oil: Y/N +1   Zone: Y/N +3

Penalties: -1 Legumes, -2 Dairy, -3 Grains, -4 Sugary or Fried Food

Deductions:	
Total:	

Start the day with 10 Points: To keep your 10 points you must eat like a true hunter gatherer; nothing but meat, fish, eggs, veggies, fruit, nuts and seeds. Add/subtract bonuses and penalties for total score.

Meal/Time	Protein	Carbs	Fat
1.			
2.			
3.			
4.			
5.			

Water: Y/N +1   WOD: Y/N +1   Fish Oil: Y/N +1   Zone: Y/N +3

Penalties: -1 Legumes, -2 Dairy, -3 Grains, -4 Sugary or Fried Food

Deductions:	
Total:	

Start the day with 10 Points: To keep your 10 points you must eat like a true hunter gatherer; nothing but meat, fish, eggs, veggies, fruit, nuts and seeds. Add/subtract bonuses and penalties for total score.

Meal/Time	Protein	Carbs	Fat
1.			
2.			
3.			
4.			
5.			

Water: Y/N +1   WOD: Y/N +1   Fish Oil: Y/N +1   Zone: Y/N +3

Penalties: -1 Legumes, -2 Dairy, -3 Grains, -4 Sugary or Fried Food

Deductions:	
Total:	

Start the day with 10 Points: To keep your 10 points you must eat like a true hunter gatherer; nothing but meat, fish, eggs, veggies, fruit, nuts and seeds. Add/subtract bonuses and penalties for total score.

Meal/Time	Protein	Carbs	Fat
1.			
2.			
3.			
4.			
5.			

Water: Y/N +1   WOD: Y/N +1   Fish Oil: Y/N +1   Zone: Y/N +3

Penalties: -1 Legumes, -2 Dairy, -3 Grains, -4 Sugary or Fried Food

Deductions:	
Total:	

Start the day with 10 Points: To keep your 10 points you must eat like a true hunter gatherer; nothing but meat, fish, eggs, veggies, fruit, nuts and seeds. Add/subtract bonuses and penalties for total score.

Meal/Time	Protein	Carbs	Fat
1.			
2.			
3.			
4.			
5.			

Water: Y/N +1   WOD: Y/N +1   Fish Oil: Y/N +1   Zone: Y/N +3

Penalties: -1 Legumes, -2 Dairy, -3 Grains, -4 Sugary or Fried Food

Deductions:	
Total:	

Start the day with 10 Points: To keep your 10 points you must eat like a true hunter gatherer; nothing but meat, fish, eggs, veggies, fruit, nuts and seeds. Add/subtract bonuses and penalties for total score.

"If you are not willing to risk the unusual, you will have to settle for the ordinary"

~ Jim Rohn

LIST OF COMMON GRAINS TO AVOID

- Whole wheat flour
- Whole rye flour
- Brown rice flour
- Millet
- Spelt flour
- Buckwheat flour
- Popcorn
- Whole wheat crackers
- Whole rice crackers
- Corn chips
- Granola bars
- Brown rice
- Wild rice
- Kasha (whole grain buckwheat)
- Quinoa
- Wheatberries
- Bulgur (cracked wheat)
- Steel cut oats
- Rolled oats

- Barley
- Buckwheat
- Granola
- Grape Nuts
- Cheerios
- Kashi Instant Hot Cereal
- Shredded Wheat
- Whole wheat
- Brown rice
- Amaranth
- Quinoa
- Corn
- Sliced bread
- Bagels
- Tortillas
- English muffins
- Pita bread
- Dinner rolls or other buns

LIST OF LEGUMES TO AVOID

- Alfalfa
- Asparagus Bean
- Asparagus Pea
- Baby Lima Bean
- Black Bean
- Black-eyed Peas
- Black Turtle Bean
- Boston Bean
- Boston Navy Bean
- Broad Bean
- Cannellini Bean
- Chickpeas
- Chili Bean
- Coco Bean
- Cranberry Bean
- Dwarf Beans
- Egyptian Bean
- Egyptian White Broad Bean
- English Bean
- Fava Bean
- Fava Coceira
- Field Pea
- French Green Beans
- Frijol Bola Roja
- Frijole Negro
- Great Northern Bean
- Green Beans
- Green and Yellow Peas
- Kidney Beans
- Lentils
- Lespedeza
- Licorice
- Lima Bean
- Madagascar Bean
- Mexican Black Bean
- Mexican Red Bean
- Molasses Face Bean
- Mung Bean
- Mung Pea
- Mungo Bean
- Navy Bean
- Pea Bean
- Peanuts
- Peruvian Bean
- Pinto Bean
- Red Bean
- Red Clover
- Red Eye Bean
- Red Kidney Bean
- Rice Bean
- Runner Bean
- Scarlet Runner Bean
- Small Red Bean
- Snow Peas
- Southern Peas
- Sugar Snap Peas
- Soybean
- Wax Bean
- White Clover
- White Kidney Bean
- White Pea Bean

PALEO/ZONE FOOD BLOCKS

Protein (cooked quantity)

chicken breast - 1 oz.

turkey breast - 1 oz.

ground turkey – 1.5 oz.

veal - 1 oz.

beef - 1 oz.

ground beef – 1.5 oz.

Canadian bacon - 1 oz.

corned beef - 1 oz.

duck - 1.5 oz.

ham - 1 oz.

lamb - 1 oz.

ground lamb – 1.5 oz.

pork -1 oz.

ground pork - 1.5 oz.

calamari - 1.5 oz.

catfish -1.5 oz.

clams- 1.5 oz.

crabmeat - 1.5 oz.

flounder/sole - 1.5 oz.

lobster - 1.5 oz.

salmon - 1.5 oz.

sardines - 1 oz.

scallops - 1.5 oz.

swordfish - 1.5 oz.

shrimp - 1.5 oz.

tuna steak - 1.5 oz.

canned tuna 1 oz.

protein powder 1 oz.

seitan 1 oz.

whole egg - 1 large

egg whites - 2 large

Carbohydrate (cooked)

artichoke - 1 small

asparagus - 12 spears

green beans - 1 cup

beet greens – 1.25 cup

black beans - 1/4 cup

bok choy - 3 cups

broccoli - 1 1/4 cup

brussel sprouts - 3/4 cup

cabbage - 1 1/3 cup

cauliflower - 1 1/4 cup

collard greens - 1 1/4 cup

dill pickles - 3 (3 in)

eggplant - 1 1/2 cup

kale - 1 1/4 cup

leeks - 1 cup

lentils - 1/4 cup

okra - 3/4 cup

onions - 1/2 cup

sauerkraut -1 cup

spaghetti squash - 1 cup

spinach - 1 1/3 cup

Swiss chard - 1 1/4 cup

tomato sauce - 1/2 cup

tomatoes - 3/4 cup

yellow squash - 1 1/4 cup

zucchini - 1 1/3 cup

Carbohydrate (raw)

broccoli - 2 cups

cabbage - 2 1/4 cups

cauliflower - 2 cups

celery - 2 cups

cucumber - 1 (9 in)

lettuce, Iceberg - 1 head

lettuce, romaine - 6 cups

mushrooms - 3 cups

onion - 2/3 cup

peppers - 1 1/4 cup

radishes - 2 cups

salsa - 1/2 cups

spinach - 4 cups

tomato - 1 cup

apple - ½

grapes - 1/2 cup

grapefruit - 1/2

honeydew - 1/2

kiwi - 1

lemon - 1

lime - 1

nectarine - 1/2

orange - 1/2

peach - 1

pear - 1/2

pineapple - 1/2 cup

plum - 1

raspberries - 2/3 cup

strawberries - 1 cup

tangerine - 1

watermelon - 2/4 cup

apple sauce - 3/8 cup

apricots - 3 small

blackberries - 1/2 cup

cantaloupe - 1/4

cherries - 7

fruit cocktail - 1/3 cup

blueberries - 1/2 cup

Fat (quantity)

almonds ~3

avocado - 1 Tbsp.

macadamia nuts ~1

olives ~5

cashews ~3

olive oil - 1/3 tsp.

tahini - 1/3 tsp.

guacamole - 1/2 Tbsp.

mayonnaise - 1/3 tsp.

sesame oil - 1/3 tsp.

sunflower seeds - 1/4 tsp.

RESOURCES

Works Cited

Wolf, Robb, *The Paleo Solution: The Original Human Diet,* 2010 Victory Belt Publishing

Barry Sears, Ph. D., *Mastering the Zone,* 1997 Harper Collins

Greg Glassman, Ph. D., http://www.crossfit.com/cf-download/Foundations.pdf, CrossFit Journal

Websites for Paleo Recipes

www.nomnompaleo.com

www.everdaypaleo.com

http://crossfitlimitless.com/recipes/

www.paleoomg.com

www.fastpaleo.com

Paleo Recipe Books

Julie and Charles Mayfield, *Paleo Comfort Foods,* 2011 Victory Belt Publishing

Misc

Do you have a great Paleo recipe? Send it to us at Stacie@crossfitlimitless.com.

Did this book help you? Send your "before" and "after" pictures and reviews to brian@crossfitlimitless.com